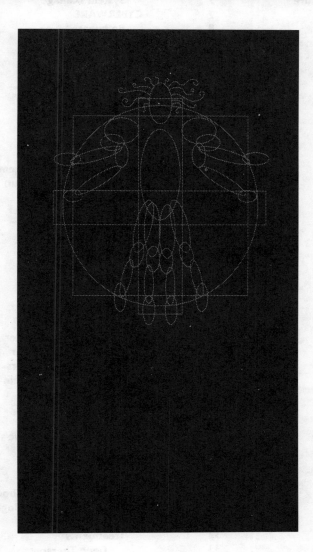

SHADOWTECH

TABLE OF CONTENTS

INTRODUCTION	4
Using This Book	4
Gaming Notes	4
BIONETICS	5
Implantation and Repair	6
Biosystem Overstress	7
Human/Metahuman Infrastructure	7
Circulatory System	7
Endocrine System	8
Lymphatic System	8
Nervous System	9
Respiratory System	10
Skin	11
Structural Systems	11
Other Major Organs	11
Secondhand Parts	12
Standard Replacement Parts	12
BIOWARE	13
Circulatory	14
Platelet Factory	14
Symbiotes	15
Synthacardium	16
Dermal	17
Orthoskin	17
Tailored Pheromones	18
Endocrine	19
Adrenal Pump	19
Suprathyroid Gland	20
Hepatic	21
Toxin Extractor	21
Lymphatic	22
Pathogenic Defense	22
Neural	23
Cerebral Booster	23
Damage Compensator	24
Mnemonic Enhancer	25
Pain Editor	26
Reflex Recorder	27
Synaptic Accelerator	28
Trauma Damper	29
Renal	30
Nephritic Screen	30
Respiratory	31
Extended Volume	31
Toxin Exhaler	32
Tracheal Filter	33
Structural	34
Enhanced Articulation	34
Muscle Augmentation	35
CYBERTECHNOLOGY	36
The Mechanical Advantage	36
Human/Machine Interface	37

Cybernetic Subsystems	37
Bodyware	37
Headware	37
Matrixware	38
Senseware	38
Cybersystem Implementation	39
System Damage	39
CYBERWARE	41
Bodyware	42
Bone Lacing	42
Hydraulic Jack	43
Headware	44
Memory	44
Datajack	45
Softlink	46
Skillwire Plus	47
Skillsofts	48
Encephalon	49
SPU (Data Management)	50
SPU (Input/Output)	51
SPU (Math)	52
Tactical Computer	53
Matrixware	54
MPCP	54
Persona Module	55
Hardening	56
Memory/Storage	57
Transfer	58
Response	59
Senseware	60
Chemical Analyzer	60
Gas Spectrometer	61
Olfactory Boosters	62
Orientation System	63
EUGENICS/GENETICS	64
The Stranger Within	64
Genetic Engineering	65
The Genome Initiative	67
The Metagene	68
The Magus Factor	70
Applied Genetics	70
Monoclonal Antibodies	70
Gengineered Biologicals	71
GENE-TECH	73
Treatments	74
Gene Therapy	74
Immunization	75
Leónization	76
Microbiologicals	77
Antibac	77
Binder	78
Zeta-Interferon	79

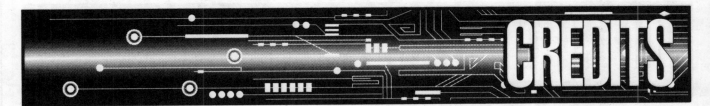

CREDITS

Doom	80
Gamma-Anthrax	81
Myco-protein	82
CHEMISTRY	83
Applied Industrial Chemistry	83
Optical Chips	83
Superconductors	84
Pharmaceuticals	85
Stimulants	85
Tranquilizers	86
Hallucinogens	86
Substance Use/Abuse	87
COMPOUNDS	89
Industrial	90
Carcerands	90
Dikote™	91
DMSO	92
Ares Squirt	92
Oxygenated Fluorocarbons	93
Ruthenium Polymers	94
ACTH	95
Atropine	96
Cyanide	97
Hyper	98
Kamikaze	99
MAO	100
TECHNOLOGY AND THE LAW	101
Availability	101
Legality	103
Restricted Items	103
Criminal Offenses	105
Criminal Charges	105
Reduced Charges	106
Jurisdiction	106
Sentencing and Punishment	107
EQUIPMENT TABLE	109

Writing
Karl Wu (who's responsible for the science)

Development
Tom Dowd (who's not)

Editorial Staff
Senior Editor
Donna Ippolito
Assistant Editor
Sharon Turner Mulvihill

Playtesters
Michael E. Colton, Mark Costello, David H. Hixon,
Bryant Wu (no relation, honest)

Production Staff
Art Director, Project Manager, Cover Design:
Jeff Laubenstein
Cover Art
David Dorman
Color Illustrations:
Brian Petersen, Joel Biske, Karl Wu, Jeff Laubenstein
Color Page Design
Jeff Laubenstein, Joel Biske
Illustration
Petersen Design, Joel Biske, Karl Wu,
Jeff Laubenstein, Dan Smith
Technical Advisor
Jill Whyte
Layout
Tara Gallagher

Some of the images in this product were created using actual Magnetic Resonance Imagery scans.

The author would like to thank all the staff at FASA, Cheryl Freedman, Michelle and Tom, Alexander von Thorn, the Worldhouse regulars, the Peanut Gallery (Mark Chaffe, Mark Ferguson, Paul Hume, and John Lee), and Circe, for their: understanding, advice, help, support, incessant badgering, constant nit-picking, and unexpected ankle-biting. Without them, writing this book wouldn't have been half the wonderful ordeal that it turned out to be.

And a special "Don't Shoot! Don't Shoot!" to the members of the illustrious GenCon '91 breakfast/dinner club. Next time it's someone else's turn.

DEDICATION

To my father, who showed me the wonders of science, and to my mother, who would've killed me had I not decided to become a doctor. Thank you.

Published by FASA Corporation • P.O. Box 6930 • Chicago, IL 60680

Technology has always been a race to stay as many steps ahead of the next guy as possible. After all, nobody wants to look at the world from the bottom of the heap. Inevitably, then, science advances ever onward in a series of oneupmanship" contests—a vicious circle called progress.

Luckily, shadowrunners are just the kind of people most likely to benefit from the fallout of such behavior, profiting both from the act of acquiring sensitive data for others and from the wealth of new tech items available at the retail end of the chain.

Shadowtech is a sourcebook for use with the **Shadowrun** game system. Its purpose is twofold. First, it explains the science underlying the latest technological discoveries leading to the development of new bioware and cyberware as well as other useful equipment . It also provides descriptions and game information for many of those same high-tech items. Second, understanding how things work not only enriches the game ambiance, but also gives both players and gamemasters a better grasp on applications and limitations inherent in the new enhancements and gear their characters will now have at their disposal.

USING THIS BOOK

The sciences covered in this book are bionetics, cybertechnology, eugenics/genetics, and chemistry. Each is divided into two sections: technology and equipment. The technology chapter examines the science in the context of current theory, general rules, techniques, and also investigates the breadth and limitations of advances made in that field of study. These sections are for gamemasters and interested players. They explain some of the science behind the mechanics, and present a more concrete picture of the level of technology available in the **Shadowrun** universe. An equipment chapter directly follows each technology section, with descriptions of items developed from that particular science. The equipment chapters introduce the game concepts of Availability Codes, Legality Ratings, and Street Indexes for "purchasable" merchandise.

An item's Legality Rating expresses how legal it is to possess a particular item. The Availability Code indicates how difficult it is to obtain the item. The Street Index indicates how to determine the "street price" for the item. For full information on Legality, Availability, and Street ratings, see p. xx in the **Technology and the Law** chapter of this book.

Nuyen costs listed with each equipment description are accurate only for legitimate and corporate buyers—usually those with licenses and permits. For rules governing permit availability costs, refer to p. x of the **Technology and the Law**) If the purchase is being made on the street or on the shadow market, multiply the listed cost by the Street Index. (Note that some items are indeed cheaper on the streets.) As usual, certain transactions may permit bargaining. If the negotiations are successful, each extra success from the Opposed Negotiation Test reduces the purchase cost by 5 percent—but the price can never fall to less than 75 percent of the published price. A Street Index of "0" means that the item in question is *never* available on the street or on the shadow market, and may only be purchased from legitimate sources.

Shadowtech also includes a comprehensive Equipment Table, p. 109, that includes all the new items described in this book as well as all equipment described in previously published **Shadowrun** products. This table gives the Legality Ratings, Availability Codes, and Street Indexes for both the new and previously described equipment.

GAMING NOTES

From behind the closed doors of the major movers and shakers in the high-tech industries to the dark corners and alleyways that define the shadow world of the runners, the information gathered here is as good as it's gonna get—at this price. But before players characters go running off to fill in the missing pieces, the gamemaster should caution them to remember what happened to the proverbial cat that got too curious.

Gamemasters should also note that one of the most important restraints on the proliferation of the technology seen in **Shadowtech** is financial. Gamemasters who run nuyen-rich games may wish to increase the Availability Ratings of items that might unbalance their games. As always, the individual gamemaster is the final arbiter of what it and is not available in a particular **Shadowrun** game. Gamemasters may wish to slowly introduce the new technology to the streets as it filters down from the higher places. It is also recommended that beginning characters not be allowed to start the game with technology from this book. Let them earn it.

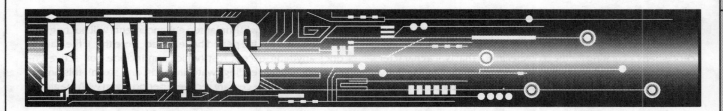

BIONETICS

"The human body is a marvel of biological design and function—Mother Nature's crowning achievement."
—Cranston's Guide to Human and Metahuman Physiology, 4th edition, 2051

"I've got a few tricks Mother Nature missed."
—Dr. Kristine Martin, Director of Research, Universal Omnitech

"...backed into a corner and surrounded by five Rippers. Am I worried? Drek, no! I've got my Doc Martin™ implants and six rounds left in my gun!"
—From a trideo ad, 2052

The human body is a complex and intricate machine built from organic materials and compounds. Just as with any other machine, man continually seeks to improve it beyond the factory specifications. Bionetics, a subset of biotechnology, is the field of science dedicated to improving the human machine on an organic level and on a macrobiological scale. That is, bionetics research seeks to improve the body's many existing organs and subsystems by enhancing and augmenting them.

Although the application of bionetics can make the body perform far beyond its original parameters, these enhancements are quite different from those possible through cybernetics. Metal is stronger and silicon faster than flesh, but flesh is more malleable. Meat is by far the subtler, and infinitely more diverse, medium.

Bioware is undetectable, except by intensive medical examination. Casual searches, X-ray scans, and the like cannot discern the difference between an augmented organ and the original. (New replacement organs, glands, and so on can be detected by examining an X-ray result, however.) Apart from exploratory surgery or other drastic measures, the only way to determine that an individual has undergone biological modification is through metabolic analysis such as a urinalysis or blood test.

Bioware, being mostly organic in composition, is less invasive than cyberware. It costs most characters no Essence Points to have bioware implanted. It is also true, however, that the body can take only so much augmentation before the delicately balanced human/metahuman metabolism begins to suffer. The maximum amount of bioware that a given individual can safely accept is represented by the *Body Index*, which is equal to the total number of Body Cost Points represented by his bioware, up to a maximum equal to the character's natural and unaugmented Body Rating, modified only by race and Karma. (Each bioware item has a Body Cost listed with its description in the next chapter.) For example, a character acquires a piece of bioware with a Body Cost of 1. Once the bioware has been successfully implanted, the character has a Body Index of 1. His maximum Body Index is equal to his unaugmented Body Rating.

As physical integrity is even more crucial for the magically active (magicians and adepts), these characters must spend Essence and add to their Body Index when selecting bioware. (An adept may factor in magically acquired attribute bonuses when calculating his or her Body Index.) The Essence cost for bioware is equal to the Body Cost. In all cases, the Body Index is merely an indicator; no "real" Body is ever actually lost in acquiring bioware.

>>>>>[Don't believe all the hype you hear or read about bioware development. Sure we've got a lot of good products, but we've got a lot of good marketing people, too. Bionetics research is a very costly endeavor and a lot of stuff is brought to market early in order to recoup some of that substantial investment immediately. Far too early, in some cases.]<<<<<
—KAM <13:27:02/11-30-52>

>>>>>[We?! What are we? Royalty?]<<<<<
—Feral <14:50:21/11-30-52>

>>>>>[No. We are the research and development team at Universal Omnitech.]<<<<< °
—KAM <19:22:08/11-30-52>

Both cyberware and bioware can be integrated within the same body. Treat bioware augmentations as base attributes in all cases (including when figuring astral space attributes), except when calculating for the bioware limit. (That is, if a character with a Body Rating 4 gets some bioware that modifies the Body Rating by +1, he still has a Body Index of 4, and not 5.)

IMPLANTATION AND REPAIR

Because of the intrinsically organic nature of bioware, implantation is a relatively simple process. In terms of procedural difficulty, treat any augmentation with a total Body Cost of .25 or less as cosmetic surgery (p. 144, **Shadowrun**). Consider anything between .26 and .75 as minor invasive surgery, while a total ranging from .76 to 1.5 indicates major invasive surgery. Procedures totaling more than 1.5 Body Cost Points, and/or those involving any neural bioware, count as drastic invasive surgery. Magicians and adepts who undergo drastic invasive surgery must check for Magic Attribute loss after healing. Although most individuals do not lose Essence as a result of bioware implantation, they may still lose Essence if the surgery goes awry.

Bioware that has been protein-matched and grown from the host's cellular matrix takes less of a toll on the body's functioning than does regular bioware. Such bioware is referred to as *cultured bioware*. Cultured bioware is implanted at a reduced Body Cost (the item's Body Cost multiplied by .75, a 25 percent reduction). Individual typing is complex and expensive. Though the average bioware enhancement already costs more nuyen than its cybernetic counterpart, cultured bioware is even more expensive (multiply the item's nuyen price by 4). All neural bioware is cultured bioware. Body Cost and monetary factors are already figured in to the listed values for neural bioware.

If an individual exceeds his Body Index for bioware implantation, he or she will go into system shock. While in such a state, the character must make all Body Success Tests at a Target Number +1 point higher for every point (or fraction thereof) he has exceeded his Body Index. This penalty is in effect until the Body Index returns either to 0 or to less than the character's natural, unaugmented Body Rating.

It can be a slow process for the host to fully integrate implanted bioware. Recovery time from bioware-related surgery is triple the normal period. Integration and recovery is faster for cultured bioware, however, which doubles rather than triples the recovery period. During the recovery stage, the patient must rest to allow his body to integrate the new functions. The newly implanted enhancements will not begin to function until the full period has elapsed. Note that if the patient does anything except rest (which can include non-active endeavors such as reading, watching vids, and so on), this time is added on to the necessary recovery period. Even with magically assisted healing, the full recovery time is needed to monitor and ensure the body's acceptance of the bioware.

An additional problem with bioware and magical healing is that the presence of bioware itself interferes on some level with magical healing. For magical healing on subjects with bioware, increase the target numbers by one-half the character's current Body Index, divided by 2, rounding down. No way around this problem exists at the current time, though researchers are diligently searching for a solution.

Perhaps the greatest advantage of bioware's organic nature is its capacity for self-repair. Once implanted, bioware becomes part of the host organism and is thus able to call on the body's natural repair functions to heal practically any damage. Depending on the level of damage taken, repair time can still be lengthy, however.

Damage to bioware systems can occur only on a single physical hit of Deadly severity. If the wound is Deadly, roll 1D6 and subtract 3. The result is the number of potential implants that might be damaged. Roll randomly to determine specifically what bioware is affected (repeats count as "No implant hit" for that particular die result). Note that dermal bioware cannot be damaged in this manner and so is not considered when determining possible system damage. Having determined exactly which bioware has been affected, roll 1D6 for each system to determine damage (subtract 1 from the die roll result if the implant is cultured bioware):

> 0 = None
> 1–2 = Light
> 3–4 = Moderate
> 5 = Serious
> 6 = Deadly

If a system suffers a Serious wound or greater, it will cease to function until healing has reduced the Damage Level to less than Serious. If a system takes enough hits to exceed Deadly damage, the system is destroyed. It cannot be healed, only removed and replaced. Bioware heals individually and in half the time normally required for general healing (p. 142–3, **Shadowrun**). Until the bioware is fully healed, the character receives no benefit from it.

>>>>>[Ah. So we are royalty, Dr. Martin.]<<<<<
  •—The Smiling Bandit <Strikes again!/Ha-Ha-Ha>

>>>>>[Very droll, Mr. Bandit. Seriously, folks. I don't like the idea of all this bioware being marketed before we've finished with all-out testing and final systems tweaks. Don't get me wrong. There's nothing dangerous about the bioware concept: it's shoddy execution that leads to problems and unforeseen effects.
    It's the same narrow-focus syndrome we first saw with the emergence of cyberware. Everybody is working on designing and producing better organs—but only one system at a time. No one's keeping the entire body as a unit in mind while developing. What this leads to are superb augmentations that simply don't work well in combination.
    One of my assistants recently ran some tests on two subjects with maximum physical and neural augmentation. He put them through a series of tests, each more demanding than the last. Poor bastards never knew what hit them. Maximum stress—maximum failure.

Medicine and magical healing can assist recovery. Magical healing must be performed at a level equal to the highest individual damage condition. (That is, if a target has an overall body damage of Moderate, cerebral booster damage of Light, and adrenal pump damage of Deadly, a mage must cast a Heal Deadly Wounds spell to have any effect on the subject as a whole.) The spell's Target Number is still adjusted by the presence of the bioware.

Upgrading or removing bioware may return the Body Index to previous levels. Having successfully removed the implant (following normal surgical procedures for bioware), the attending surgeon makes a Biotech (B/R) Success Test against a Target Number equal to the character's current Body Index. The number of successes (round all figures to the nearest tenth) dictate the amount of Body Index recovered:

> 0 = 10%
> 1 = 25%
> 2–3 = 45%
> 4–5 = 60%
> 6+ = 90%

If upgrading, continue with the regular implantation costs and procedures. None of the invested Body Index can be recovered if the system is destroyed by the damage sustained. Note also that some pieces of bioware, once implanted, may not be removed (e.g., neural bioware). The gamemaster has the final decision on what may or may not be removed. Essence, once lost, can never be regained (as far as anyone knows).

BIOSYSTEM OVERSTRESS

An additional complication related to bioware is what has come to be known as biosystem overstress. When certain systems or aspects of the body are artificially pushed beyond a natural limit, dysfunction may occur. The chance of overstress occurs whenever bioware has boosted an attribute beyond two times its natural value (character-generation rating plus Karmic increases). The gamemaster may call for an Overstress Resistance Test anytime that attribute is in use. Roll a number of dice equal to either the character's Body Rating or to the Attribute Rating in question, whichever is lower, against a Target Number equal to the character's current Body Index (round down). It requires only one success to prevent dysfunction and overstress. If the Success Test fails, the Attribute Rating immediately drops to one-half its natural value and the character takes a Moderate Stun wound. The fatigue damage will heal normally, while the reduced Attribute Ratings are regained at a rate of 1 point per hour of rest.

HUMAN/METAHUMAN INFRASTRUCTURE

Bioware cannot operate in a vacuum. Unlike cybernetic components, bioware augmentations are little more than configurations of cells and chemical processes unless implanted in a physical body. Biological prosthetics are also more difficult to design and execute than is cyberware. Bioware must be integrated into the body's own workings as if it were an original feature.

While a cybertechnician can afford to use the "bigger hammer" technique to perform body enhancement, a biotechnician cannot. With an instrument as finely tuned as the body, even the slightest change in status can result in drastic and unwanted side effects.

With the need for such finesse, the designer of bioware must study and understand each of the body's subsystems and organs before he can create successful and non-damaging biological equipment.

CIRCULATORY SYSTEM

The body's system for circulating oxygen and nutrients and for the removal of carbon dioxide and cellular wastes is essential to life. The circulatory system and the heart are what make possible the complex organism that is human life.

On average, the heart is a small, muscular organ weighing approximately 283.5 to 311.9 grams. Each beat of the heart pumps roughly 147.9 milliliters of blood through the heart. At a rate of about 70 beats per minute for the average adult (105,000 beats per day), the heart pumps more than 6,813 liters of blood through the body's 96,560.6 kilometers of blood vessels a day.

For the average human adult, normal blood volume is between 3.8 and 4.9 liters, accounting for approximately 7 percent of human/metahuman body weight. A single drop of blood contains more than 250 million separate particles and cells. Blood cells constitute roughly 40 percent of the blood's total volume, with plasma making up another 55 percent, and the remaining 5 percent comprised of free-floating proteins, sugars, salts, wastes, and such.

The three general types of blood cells are red blood cells (erythrocytes), which perform gas exchange; white blood cells (leukocytes), which defend against disease and infection; and platelets (thrombocytes), which play a key role in blood-clotting and general healing.

. Now, to be fair, these were extremely grueling situations, and hardly standard operating conditions, by any stretch of the imagination. In normal situations there should be no real problems.]<<<<<
—KAM <18: 57:34/12-01:52>

>>>>>[Normal operating conditions, eh? Doc, have you ever been so deep in the drek that everything is pumping and spinning and snapping at once? No chance to rest, no chance to breathe?]<<<<<
—Winger <23:11:40/12-01-52>

>>>>>[No. Sorry, but I prefer less terminal pursuits.]<<<<<
—KAM <12:01:33/12-02-52>

Augmentation of the circulatory system takes place on two levels: in the heart itself and in the blood's many components. In general, it is not so much the system that needs enhancement as does what constitutes and travels in the blood.

ENDOCRINE SYSTEM

The endocrine system is a network of ductless glands that pump and/or secrete hormones into the bloodstream. Together with the nervous system, these glands coordinate most of the body's functions.

Hormones can most accurately be described as the body's chemical messengers. Producing both long- and short-term changes, they are tightly linked to the powerful emotional states of fear, anger, joy, and despair. Amazingly diverse in function, hormones range in type from growth (somatotropin) and blood-sugar control (glucagon) to steroids (testosterone and choles-terol). To date, more than a hundred human/metahuman hormones have been cataloged.

Eight glands make up the endocrine system: the hypo-thalamus (regulates body temperature, hunger, thirst, sex drive, and controls pituitary secretions), the pituitary (controls bone growth and general endocrine system activity), the pineal gland (related to reproduction), the thyroid (regulates metabolism, energy use, and body development), the parathyroid (controls calcium levels in the blood), the thymus (develops immune system in children; no discernible function in adults), the adrenals (regulate salt and water balance and also stress re-sponse), the pancreas (regulates blood sugar), and the ovaries/testes (female/male sexual development).

Because many of the functions of the endocrine system are so subtle and delicately balanced, direct glandular modification is not recommended. Only gross metabolic functions are al-tered; all other manipulations are carried out indirectly through the introduction of synthetic hormonal derivatives.

LYMPHATIC SYSTEM

Closely related to the cardiovascular system, the lymphatic system performs several major functions: filtering out disease-causing (pathogenic) organisms, manufacturing leukocytes, generating antibodies, distributing fluid and nutrients, and draining excess fluids and proteins (so tissues do not swell).

Unlike the bloodstream, lymph flows through the lym-phatic system without the assistance of any pump. As new tissue fluid drains into the spaces between the cells, it creates continuous pressure to move. Contraction and expansion of nearby arteries and muscles also aids in moving the fluid.

Lying along the vessels that make up the lymphatic system are oval clusters of lymphoid tissue called lymph nodes/glands. For the most part, these nodes are thinly scattered throughout the body, but several areas (neck, groin, and armpits) contain large clusters of the more than one hundred individual nodes. Within each node is a series of fibrous traps that act as filters; swelling of these nodes usually accompanies an inflammation, indicating that the nodes are operating beyond their normal capacity.

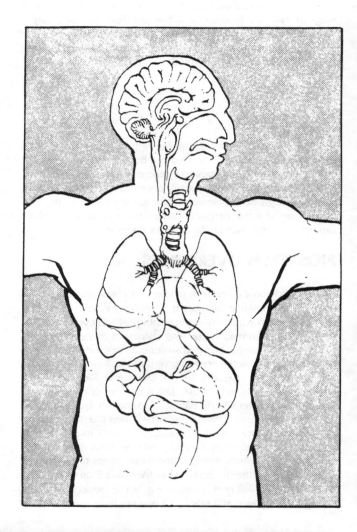

>>>>>[Drek, but don't that just make me ever so happy not to have jumped onto the bioware bandwagon.]<<<<<
—Winger <22:53:27/12-02:52>

>>>>>[Yeah, right. No need to get on the bioware bandwagon when you're already riding the cyberware express, neh? O.K., chummers, listen up. We're all in agreement that bioware still has a few bugs that desperately need ironing out. Nobody's debating the issue. What you must realize, though, is that bioware is no more dangerous than cyberware. Too much cyberware and your system geeks out—you die. Too much bioware and your body craps out—you still die. Six of one, half-dozen of the other.

Sure, there's risk involved in taking yourself to the edge, but I don't think that anyone with even a single active gray cell isn't conscious of what he or she is doing before going out to get 60 percent of the natural body replaced.

Personal augmentation isn't a simple matter of "cyberware, good; bioware, bad." It's more an issue of how far you want

The spleen is the largest body of lymphoid tissue. About the size of the heart and located on the left side behind the stomach, it is a fragile and spongy mass able to hold up to one liter of blood. The spleen filters lymph, produces leukocytes, and removes old red blood cells from the body. The spleen also serves as a blood reserve, contracting and sending its stored blood into the body in times of need. A spleen can be easily ruptured in incidents of physical trauma. Repairing the spleen is such a lengthy and, more often than not, futile, procedure that damaged spleens are more often removed and replaced. During recovery, the rest of the lymphatic system can take up most of the spleen's functions.

Bioware enhancements to the lymphatic system work toward augmenting the efficiency of the immune system. Because of the spleen's delicate nature, the organ's integrity is never breached by a surgeon's implements. Material is added to it and attached externally through the use of microsurgical units called nanites.

NERVOUS SYSTEM

The human/metahuman nervous system is a vast, bodywide network of specialized tissue. It is, without doubt, the most complex and important system in the body. Because of the delicate and fragile nature of the nervous system, microsurgical procedures are required to implement neural system augmentations.

The whole nervous system is generally divided into two linked "subsystems": the central nervous system (including the brain and the spinal cord) and the peripheral nervous system (including the somatic and autonomic systems).

Nervous tissue exists in two forms: gray and white matter. Gray matter is made up of nerve cells that originate and receive nerve impulses, while white matter consists of nerve fibers that transmit those impulses from point to point.

Structurally, the brain is a mass of nervous tissue slightly larger than a grapefruit and weighing approximately 1.4 kilograms; it is situated in the skull's cranial cavity at the upper end of the spinal cord. Functionally, the brain subdivides into a number of connected masses, each of which specializes in performing a number of functions. Among them are: the medulla oblongata (autonomic functions), the pons and cerebellum (reflex maintenance of balance and posture), the thalamus (chief sensory relay), the basal ganglia (muscle tone and motor coordination), and the cerebrum (the center of cognitive and higher functions such as memory, thought, motor function, speech, sensation, and so on).

The spinal cord, which is about 45 centimeters long and 1.25 centimeters in diameter, extends from the base of the skull to the first lumbar vertebra. It is composed almost entirely of nerve tissue, a core of gray matter surrounded by a sheath of white matter. Thirty-one pairs of spinal nerves branch out from the spinal cord at regular intervals to relay sensory impulses and motor commands to and from the central nervous system. The spine functions primarily as the major nerve trunk between the brain and all other parts of the body; its additional function is as a secondary processor for motor action.

Not all messages make the full journey to the brain and back. Level with each pair of nerves leaving the spine is an alternate system that relays impulses within the spinal cord without involving the brain. Known as the reflex arc, this mechanism is responsible for maintaining muscle tone as well as for specific muscle responses known as reflex actions. Instruction at the spinal cord level often results in the body performing an action before the brain receives and interprets the initial impulse.

A reflex action is a rapid, involuntary muscle response to sensory stimulus. Actions are classified as superficial, deep/tendon, and visceral. Superficial reflex action results from skin stimulation, as in tickling. The knee-jerk is a classic tendon reflex, while most involuntary physiological actions such as swallowing depend on visceral reflexes.

The somatic nervous system keeps the body and brain in touch with the external world and responds to stimuli. Sensory information is carried to the brain by means of the cranial nerves, and transmitted to the spine by way of the spinal nerves.

Involuntary muscles and secreting glands are controlled primarily by the autonomic nervous system, which regulates functions not under the direct control of the brain (heart-rate, blushing, sweating, digestion, and so on). The autonomic system is divided into the sympathetic nervous system and the parasympathetic nervous system.

Extreme activity of the sympathetic system mobilizes the body to cope with physical stress—dilating the pupils, raising the hair, sweating, widening the coronary and other major arteries to increase the supply of blood to the muscles, constricting peripheral capillaries, dilating the bronchi and bronchioles to facilitate gas exchange, increasing the force of the heartbeat, and decreasing the activity of the digestive organs. In sum, stimulating the endocrine system to release the hormone adrenalin.

to push it. Or, to rephrase the question: "How do you wish to die?" To which the intelligent answer would be: "I don't. Thank you very much."]<<<<<
—The Smiling Bandit <Strikes again!/Ha-Ha-Ha>

>>>>>[An intelligent response, granted, but hardly a practical one. We must all strive to make something of the hand we are dealt. Sometimes that means getting in over your head and bluffing, hoping that nobody's going to call you on it.]<<<<<
—Lightning Bug <08:32:46/12-03-52>

>>>>>[Whoa. Period. Full stop, chummers. What's all this philosophical drek? I thought this was a technical forum. The pansy stuff is down the net, three nodes over. Now, can we get back to shop talk, before I rip somebody's head off?]<<<<<
—Feral <10:03:51/12-03-52>

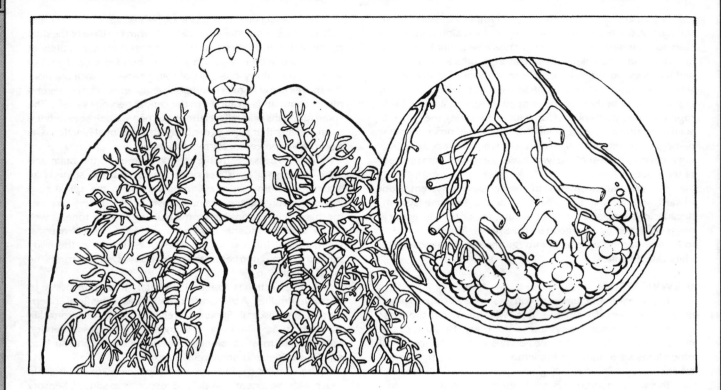

Parasympathetic nervous impulses restore the body to normal functioning levels after stress—slowing down the heart, reducing blood flow, and allowing sphincters to relax. Both the sympathetic and parasympathetic nervous systems interact closely with the endocrine system, and are greatly influenced by emotion.

Bioware designed to enhance the nervous system deals mostly with cognitive ability, motor function, and the redirection of sensory feedback. The problem of actual sensory-ability augmentation is left to cybernetic implants, which can deal more elegantly with the complications of enhanced senses (e.g., rebuilding the sensory collector, interpreting the new forms of data, and so forth). Because the nervous system is so delicate and sensitive to damage, all neural bioware must be individually cultured. The Body Cost cannot be reduced any further (cultured bioware modifiers for Body Cost are already calculated into the published figures).

RESPIRATORY SYSTEM

The lungs, and specifically the alveoli, are the sites of gas exchange: the intake of oxygen into the bloodstream and the removal of carbon dioxide from it. The average adult breathes in and out 13.1 times per minute and 18,925 times per day. Although adult human lung capacity is about 2.5 liters, lungs do not fully deflate when exhaling. An average breath only moves a tidal volume of .5 liters of air. Still, that totals more than 9,462.5 liters of air moving in and out of an average set of lungs each day.

The lungs themselves are delicate and fragile. With more than 300 million alveoli in each lung, direct manipulation of the lungs is as undesirable as it is difficult. Respiratory enhancements are made through the use of indirect modification to the breathing pattern.

Augmentations to the trachea (windpipe) are included with all other forms of respiratory system enhancement.

>>>>>[Such eloquence. Ah, to bask in the presence of the gifted…Some of us peons cannot even hope to aspire, but must instead be content to observe in awe.]<<<<<
　　—The Smiling Bandit <Strikes again!/Ha-Ha-Ha>

>>>>>[I said shop talk. Pay attention.]<<<<<
　　—Feral <21:12:48/12-03-52>

>>>>>[I understand that bioware is sort of a precursor to full-scale human gengineering.]<<<<<
　　—The Man <02:15:25/12-04-52>

>>>>>[Only in the most peripheral way. Yes, the organs must be designed and then grown using gengineering tanks. No, this process cannot be applied to humans in the same fashion.

SKIN

Skin is the body's first line of defense against the outside world, and is the body's largest and most extensive organ. Averaging only .5 millimeters in thickness, it consists of two layers, the epidermis (outermost layer) and the dermis.

The dermis, which provides the skin its nutrition, sturdiness, and resilience, is composed primarily of collagen (a fibrous protein) and elastin (the substance that gives skin its elasticity). Contained within the dermis layer are the body's sweat glands and tactile sensors.

Skin-based bioware deals with enhancing the defensive capabilities of the organ. Modifications, though long and intensive, are relatively simple and use conventional surgical methods.

STRUCTURAL SYSTEMS

The skeletal and muscular systems are grouped together under the heading of structural systems. As these systems stand, man can do very little to improve upon their design.

Structurally, bones are an amazing piece of engineering. Surrounding each bone is the periosteum, a thin layer of tissue packed with nerves and blood vessels; any sensation that seems to come from a bone actually originates in the periosteum. Under the periosteum is the bone proper, known as compact bone. Honeycombing the compact bone are thousands of tiny holes and passageways, through which run nerves and the blood vessels that supply oxygen and nutrients to the bone. It is this honeycombing feature that gives bones their remarkable strength; the femur (thigh bone) is, kilogram for kilogram, stronger than reinforced concrete, routinely resisting the 84 kg/cm^2 (1200 PSI) of impact that the body endures with every step taken. At the core of the bone is a spongy, gelatinous material called the bone marrow, which produces, variously, white blood cells, red blood cells, or platelets. The type of blood cells produced depends on the particular bone in question.

As for the body's muscular system, it is composed of three basic types of muscle tissue: voluntary (striped/striated), involuntary (smooth), and the muscles of the heart (cardiac). Striated muscles are the muscles of motion, and are capable of strong, controlled contractions. Smooth muscles line blood vessels, the stomach, digestive tract, and other internal organs. They do not contract as powerfully, nor do they generally need to. Cardiac muscle is structurally similar to both the smooth and striated types; cardiac muscles are involuntary and are some of the strongest muscles in the body.

Functionally, science can do little to improve upon the structural system's performance. Muscle tissue already uses energy six times more efficiently than any combustion system, and to breach the integrity of bone would be akin to putting deliberate cracks in a building's load-bearing frame.

Bioenhancement of the body's structural system focuses on reinforcing rather than rebuilding, and on manipulating the non-structural components within the system (i.e., bone marrow).

OTHER MAJOR ORGANS

The only other body parts that are involved in system augmentation are the kidneys and the liver.

The kidneys are a set of paired organs that filter the blood, removing waste products and reclaiming water, sugar, salt, and potassium, among other vital substances. These small organs process and cleanse the total volume of blood in the body every 50 minutes; more than 1,710 liters of blood are pumped through the kidneys every day. The actual filtering is performed in small, tube-like structures called nephrons. Each kidney contains more than a million nephrons.

Kidney augmentation involves fine-tuning the sensitivity of the nephrons. Because it is easier to grow a new kidney to specification than to surgically alter it, kidney enhancements usually involve removing the original organs and transplanting a whole new pair of "vat-grown" replacements.

Weighing in at roughly 1.4 kilograms, the liver is the largest organ inside the body. The liver can continue to function even when as much as 90 percent is removed. Given enough time, the remaining 10 percent fragment would probably grow back to its original size. One of the most important organs in the body, the liver is the main site for catabolism (the breakdown of complex substances such as starches into sugars, proteins into amino acids, and so on) and anabolism (the chemical conversion of substances, such as constructing glucose from "free-floating" hydrocarbons). Aside from its metabolic contributions to the body, the organ also stores vitamins, aids in digestion, maintains blood sugar level, and filters toxins from the bloodstream.

Altering the metabolic functions of the liver is not recommended. It is far easier and safer to effect metabolic rate changes by modifying the endocrine system (which regulates metabolic activity). Bioware for the liver concentrates more on the filtration and the detoxification abilities rather than the metabolic features. Because the liver is relatively durable and versatile, augmentation is a relatively simple and safe procedure.

When bioware is grown, the altered genetic commands are designed optimally to produce the augmented organ. Nothing else is a concern. In this process, the rest of the growth medium (i.e., host body) may undergo all sorts of side effects that would hamper normal human development. The coding is developed to promote maximally efficient creation of the organ. The rest of the host is superficial (and usually broken down and recycled after the organ has been harvested.)

As you can see, gengineering cannot apply the same hack-and-slash techniques toward human eugenics.]<<<<<
—KAM <13:06:31/12-04-52>

>>>>>[Um, what do you mean "host body"?]<<<<<
—Cobra <19:17:31/12-04-52>

>>>>>[I mean exactly that—a body. Organs and body parts (including standard replacement parts) have to come from somewhere.

SECONDHAND PARTS

With the cost of original bioware so high, it is no surprise that a market for secondhand bioware has developed. Usually selling for 40 percent to 60 percent less than original parts, the "used" bioware has the same Body Costs as the new. Some of this bioware is sold by the original owner, but some of it is "acquired" by more nefarious means. This latter means is known as organlegging.

A piece of secondhand bioware will behave in a relatively normal manner (depending on the gamemaster)—until it suffers damage. Because the transplanted bioware is not implanted in the intended user, it tends to suffer from trauma at a more prodigious rate. Add +1 to die rolls when making Damage Tests for secondhand bioware. On a result of 7, that particular piece of bioware is considered "destroyed"; it is no longer functional and cannot be repaired, only removed and replaced (see **Implantation and Repair**, above, for more details).

Though a market exists for "generic" secondhand bioware, cultured bioware has no equivalent market. Bioware is usually homogeneous in its cellular nature and makeup. It is genetically "indifferent," precluding the problem of possible rejection by the host body. Cultured bioware is, by definition, the exact opposite—protein-typed and altered to match its intended owner down to the genetic core.

Once removed from the body, cultured bioware has no further function except as a source of recyclable materials. Generic bioware can be sold to organleggers or body shops for 5 percent to 30 percent of its original cost (the result of 1D6 multiplied by 5 percent). Prices are negotiable, but may never rise to higher than 30 percent of the original cost.

STANDARD REPLACEMENT PARTS

The advances in biotechnology have had a profound impact on the buying and selling of standard (unenhanced) body parts to replace those lost through physical/magical trauma or ill health. With the proliferation of quality bionetics, prices for "vat-issue" body parts have fallen dramatically; growth time has also been reduced.

Forced Growth multiplies the Body Part cost by its Growth Rating (choose up to a maximum of 10), and divides growth time by this rating.

The following table replaces the corresponding rules on pp. 145–46 of the first edition **Shadowrun** rules.

REPLACEMENT PARTS TABLE

Body Part	Base Time	Base Price
Small organ	3 weeks	7,500¥
Large organ	5 weeks	15,000¥
Hand/Foot	6 weeks	15,000¥
Limb	8 weeks	25,000¥

Grade	Availability	Compatibility	Price
Clonal	Must be grown	100%	Base x 2
Type O	50%	90%	Base
Type G	75%	75%	Base x 0.8
Secondhand	100%	3D6 x 5%	Base x 0.4

The Compatibility of a Forced Growth Part is reduced by twice its Growth Rate.

Compatibility	Failure Under Stress
100%	No chance
90–99%	1 in 6
70–89%	2 in 6
40–69%	3 in 6
01–39%	4 in 6

You can't just grow an eyeball, or a heart, or a kidney. You have to cultivate the entire body as a unit and then take what you need. The rest you recycle for next time.]<<<<<
　　—KAM <07:50:14/12-05-52>

>>>>>[Aw wiz. . .I just had an eye replaced. I don't feel so good. . . .]<<<<<
　　—Cobra <18-46-42/12-05-52>

>>>>>[Well, at least you don't get those animal-rights protestors anymore.]<<<<<
　　—Ludwig the Mad <20:12:51/12-05-52>

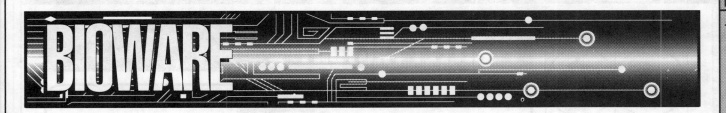

BIOWARE

"Igor, I think I've created a monster..."
—Doctor Victor Frankenstein, in the film **Frankenstein**

"The brain? From some Abby person...Abby Normal, I think..."
—Igor, in the film **Young Frankenstein**

Think of bioware as biological cyberware. Bioware represents the pinnacle of modern medical technology, but it's still in the testing stages. Because of that, some problems do exist in the application of bioware. Most problems stem from inadequate field-testing or unforeseen long-term effects, which are only showing up now because bioware is such a recent development.

The gamemaster is free to make bioware products as reliable or as quirky as desired (though not so unreliable that he penalizes players unnecessarily).

What follows are descriptions of bioware products available to the general public as of summer 2052.

>>>>>[Frag this "field testing" drek. Face it, chummers. The man means guinea pigs.]<<<<<
    —Lab Rat <19:01:36/12-05-52>

ORDER HERE

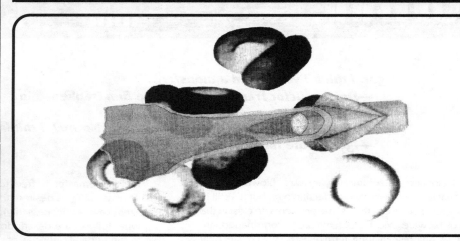

RATINGS

Legality Rating: **Legal**

Availability: **5/8 days**

Street Index: **1.5**

PLATELET FACTORY

Platelet factories increase the body's ability to handle damage.

By selective enhancement, thrombocyte (platelet) production within bone marrow is increased to a high level, resulting in the formation of "platelet factories." When the character takes physical damage, the increased level of platelets in the bloodstream stops bleeding at the site, lessening the trauma from large wounds. A platelet factory removes 1 point of Moderate or higher physical damage. That is, a character implanted with platelet factories would mark off only 5 boxes on the Physical Condition Monitor for a Serious wound, rather than the usual 6.

The high concentration of platelets in the bloodstream can present the risk of thrombosis (the clotting/coagulation of blood within living blood vessels) and resulting embolisms, (blocking of the arteries). To counter this risk, the character must take specially tailored anticoagulants on a regular basis. If the anticoagulant is not administered, make a Body Success Test every twelve hours against a Target Number 3, applying a +1 modifier for each day the character has not taken the anticoagulant. If the test generates no successes, the character has suffered a cardiac arrest or aneurysm stemming from an embolism. Assess immediately for Deadly Physical and Mental Wounds. The anticoagulant must be taken once daily. It costs 20¥/dose for an injected formula, 25¥/dose for the orally administered form.

Body Cost	Price
.4	30,000¥

>>>>>[These things are really double-edged. They can save your butt, and they can also be a real pain in it, too.]<<<<<
—Neon Samurai <19:47:23/12-05-52>

>>>>>[I agree. A friend of mine swears by them. He told me once that those platelet factories kept him from bleeding to death in a blowout he was in. So, I got myself a set. Well, a week later I was involved in a small altercation at a local drinking establishment. Got punched out royally in the nose. Fraggin' factories stopped the bleeding so fast the blood didn't even have time to drain out. I had to go to a street doc to have my nose cleared out so I could breathe through it again. Sheesh.]<<<<<
—The Edge <22:13:07/12-05-52>

SYMBIOTES

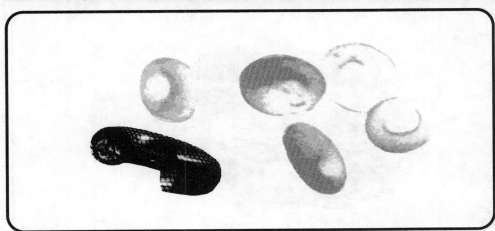

ORDER HERE

RATINGS

Legality Rating: **Legal**

Availability: **5/10 days**

Street Index: **1**

Symbiotes consist of a number of tailored microorganisms (nanites) that are introduced into the host subject's bloodstream. They so dramatically enhance the body's own regenerative functions that the host's natural healing time is reduced for physical and mental trauma. The character must, however, take in 50 percent to 100 percent more food and beverage to fuel the symbiote activity. (If the individual also has a suprathyroid gland, note that the increased food and drink requirements are cumulative. That is, a character with both Level 2 symbiotes and a suprathyroid would have to consume three times as much food and liquid as a "normal" person of his/her same race, sex, and age.) As this enhancement does not affect the stomach's capacity, the increased demand for food must be handled by either eating more often or by ingesting an expensive (triple normal food cost) diet of tailored nutrients.

If a character who has both symbiotes and a suprathyroid opts for the tailored diet, his/her total calculated food requirement is halved; the individual in the above example of symbiotes-2 and the suprathyroid would have to eat and drink only one and a half times as much as normal if taking the tailored nutrients. Lost blood volume due to physical trauma and bleeding does not offset symbiote functioning unduly. The symbiotes will regenerate and grow in number along with the replenishing blood supply.

Level	% of Normal Healing Time	Food/Beverage Intake	Body Cost	Price
1	90%	+50%	.4	15,000¥
2	70%	+70%	.7	35,000¥
3	50%	+100%	1	60,000¥

>>>>>[Hey, chummers, these things are great for getting over the cold or the flu. You come down with the bug, but a day or two later, the symbiotes have cleaned it out of your system!]<<<<<
—Spot <01:18:18<02/12-06-52>

>>>>>[Symbiotes may be useful and all, but drek, have you seen the kind of spectacle you make? Constantly eating or drinking, pockets full of food and munchies. Big-time bovine, chummer. Helpful, sure, but *trés non-chic, mes amis.*]<<<<<
—Vince Vatman <03:21:57/12-06-52>

SYNTHACARDIUM

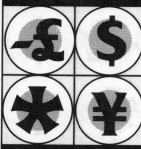

ORDER HERE

RATINGS

Legality Rating: **Legal**

Availability: **4/10 days**

Street Index: **1.5**

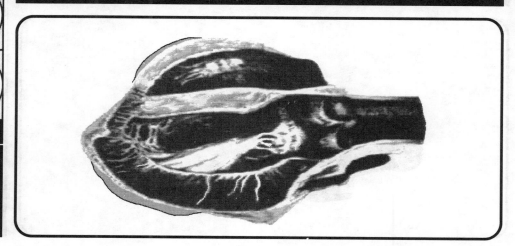

Synthacardium boosts the heart's capabilities by boosting its ability to handle increased levels of activity.

Synthacardium consists of artificially enhanced myocardium, the muscle tissue that makes up the heart. When added to the structure of the heart, it enables the organ to perform at higher levels of strenuous activity with greater ease. Each level of synthacardium adds +1 die to Athletics-based Success Tests and tasks. The character also becomes less prone to diseases of the heart and other cardiac-related problems. Characters receive an extra die for each level of synthacardium in their heart for all for tests to resist cardiac and circulatory-based conditions or ailments. (If a Level 1 synthacardium recipient also has a platelet factory, but is without his anticoagulant, he must add 2 dice to his rolls to resist the ill-effects.)

Level	Additional Dice	Body Cost	Price
1	+1	.2	6,000¥
2	+2	.3	15,000¥

>>>>>[I've been told there are some potentially nasty side effects that go along with adding synthacardium to existing cardial tissue. Something about the increased strength of the heart being great for performance, but that the same strength leads to massive bruising (upped blood pressure), throbbing in the ears (again high blood pressure near the eardrum and such), and migraines near the temples.]<<<<<
—Winger <10:12:51/12-06-52>

>>>>>[A small price to pay, in my opinion.]<<<<<
—Feral <12:24:36/12-06-52>

>>>>>[Yeah, but you usually have most of those symptoms anyway, don't ya?]<<<<<
—Ludwig the Mad <13:25:19/12-06-52>

ORTHOSKIN

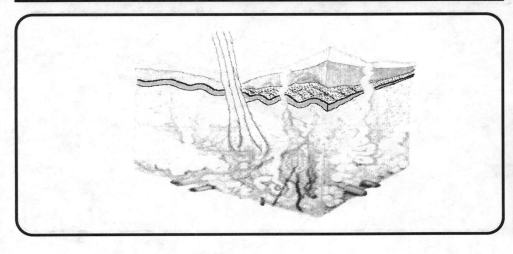

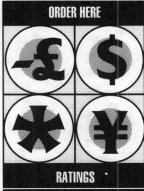

RATINGS

Legality Rating: **5P-BA**

Availability: **8/8 days**

Street Index: **.8**

Orthoskin weaves an energy-diffusing material under the skin that gives the recipient the equivalent of personal armor.

The transformation of skin into orthoskin is an extensive process. The individual's skin is peeled back section by section, and the body's dermal layer is fortified by grafts of sythagen (a strengthened and reinforced collagen-protein derivative), flextin (a synthetic and more resilient form of the elastin protein), and flakes of modified and laced cartilage. Much more durable and resistant to damage and environmental extremes, orthoskin gives a character extra levels of both impact and ballistic armor, which is cumulative with externally worn armor.

Once transplanted, orthoskin grows like normal skin and is virtually indistinguishable from unaugmented skin; the underlying subdermis is altered at the same time to enable it to sustain the new dermal architecture. An additional bonus from orthoskin is that any damage to the body heals with little or no scarring. A disadvantage is that characters with orthoskin lose some degree of sensitivity of touch because of the increased density of the dermis. To reflect this, add the orthoskin level to the Target Number for tactile-based Perception Tests (e.g., orthoskin-2 adds +2 to such a Perception Test).

Orthoskin is not compatible with dermal armor.

Level	Armor	Body Cost	Price
1	+1 Impact	.5	25,000¥
2	+1 Impact, +1 Ballistic	1	60,000¥
3	+2 Impact, +1 Ballistic	1.5	100,000¥

>>>>>[This stuff is great! Tons better than dermal armor!]<<<<<
—Toymeister <14:47:28/12-06-52>

>>>>>[Orthoskin and dermal armor are based on two entirely different design principles. Dermal armor places additional bulk beneath the skin to enable the host to withstand a wide variety of heavy physical damage. Orthoskin attempts to diffuse the energy of the trauma over the body's entire surface area, reducing the damage to a more manageable level.]<<<<<
—KAM <18:13:11/12-06-52>

>>>>>[Whatever. It works.]<<<<<
—Toymeister <20:20:20/12-06-52>

ORDER HERE

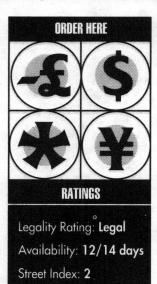

RATINGS

Legality Rating: **Legal**

Availability: **12/14 days**

Street Index: **2**

TAILORED PHEROMONES

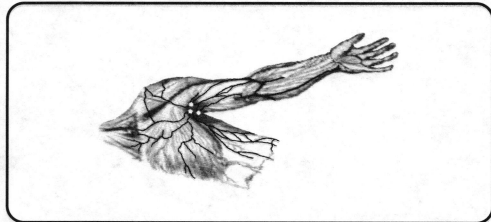

It is possible to alter an individual's main sweat glands so that they will release discrete levels of specially designed pheromones into the surrounding air. Only a few molecules of the pheromone are required to trigger the effect, but no matter how low the concentration of secreted pheromone, all persons in the area of dispersion are affected equally. Dispersion is largely dependent on atmospheric conditions.Under average conditions (an open area with little or no wind), the area of effect extends from the source of the released pheromones in a circle whose diameter is approximately 15 to 20 meters. Mild air currents can increase the area covered, but stronger winds will disperse the pheromones before they can take effect.

The effectiveness of pheromones depends on the olfactory system of the targets; pheromones have no effect on individuals with impaired olfactory abilities or those unable to use their sense of smell (e.g., astral travelers). Pheromones are also species specific; although human and metahuman pheromones are similar, pheromones will have no effect on non-humanoid creatures. (In related species, such as human to metahumans, and metahumans to different metahumans, halve the effect of the pheromones, rounding down.) Being individually discrete, pheromone augmentation continues to function even if the character is in the presence of another character with tailored pheromones. Every level of tailored pheromones adds a +1 to the recipient's Charisma and Social Skill Tests. Cultured pheromones are exceptionally powerful; double the normally acquired benefits, and extend ranges by an additional 50 percent.

Tailored pheromones have no effect on astral or conjuring abilities and skills.

Level	Bonus	Body Cost	Price
1	+1 Charisma/Social Skill dice	.4	20,000¥
2	+2 Charisma/Social Skill dice	.6	45,000¥

>>>>>[Hey, aren't pheromones sex-dependent?]<<<<<
　　—Feral <22:17:11/12-06-52>

>>>>>[Most pheromones are, indeed, targeted at the opposite gender. Other pheromones, however, are used as "territorial markers" and "presence scents." These pheromones can be used to establish a zone of "dominance." The alterations accompanying the tailoring process are full-spectrum—all the secreted pheromones are boosted, not just the sex-oriented ones.]<<<<<
　　—KAM <23:01:42/12-06-52>

>>>>>[Oh. Too bad.]<<<<<
　　—Feral <23-17-52/12-06-52>

>>>>>[Very subtle, too. You usually can't tell you're being influenced.]<<<<<
　　—The Smiling Bandit <Strikes sgain!/Ha-Ha-Ha>

ADRENAL PUMP

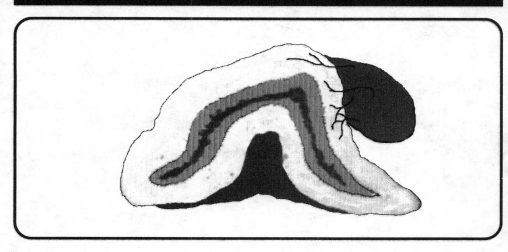

Legality Rating: **5P-BB**

Availability: **10/16 days**

Street Index: **3**

The adrenal pump is a small, muscular sac implanted in the lower abdominal cavity and connected to each of the two suprarenal (or adrenal) glands. When dormant, the pump concentrates and serves as a reservoir for the hormones adrenaline and noradrenaline. When activated, the sac contracts, sending a surge of concentrates into the bloodstream. Stress and other emotional states such as anger, fear, or lust will also activate the pump.

As the effects produced by hormones depend both on the amount secreted and the responsiveness of the organ or tissue in question, the actual combat effectiveness of the adrenal pump is variable. Once active, roll 1D6 for each level of the adrenal pump; the die result indicates the number of turns the hormones stay in the blood, and, therefore, the number of turns the bonuses will apply. Each level of the pump adds +1 to Quickness, +2 to Strength, +1 to Willpower, and +2 to Reaction for as long as the concentrates remain in the bloodstream. (Quickness raised in this manner does not also affect Reaction.) When that time has expired, however, the subject takes Deadly mental damage with a Power Level equal to one-half the number of turns the hormones remained in the blood (round down) and a Staging of 2 because of system shock and fatigue. For example, after four rounds of hormone-activation, the attack would be 2D2. The character may roll Body dice to resist the damage.

Once the adrenal pump has discharged its load, it takes approximately 10 to 15 minutes (9 + 1D6) for the pump to regenerate its supply. If the pump activates before the sac has been refilled, halve the regular number of turns active (but not the fatigue after-effects). The pump cannot discharge more than once during the same encounter. Studies have shown that high levels of adrenalin and noradrenaline in the bloodstream contribute to high blood pressure; speculation based on available data also points toward higher incidences of cardiac-related problems stemming from long-term use. When the pump is working, subjects are also more prone to critical heart failure through sheer overexertion. If a character whose adrenal pump is activated completely fails a Body Success Test (rolling all ones), he suffers immediate cardiac arrest (heart attack/Deadly physical and mental damage).

Although normally triggered involuntarily, the adrenal pump can also be triggered on demand through the use of adrenocorticotropic hormone (ACTH/corticotrophin); inhalers with six doses can be acquired from various sources (see **Compounds**, p. xx, for more details).

The Reaction increase does not affect the skills involved in rigging or decking. To activate or resist the activation of the pump, the character makes a Willpower (6) Test. A Light wound of any kind automatically activates the pump, assuming the character is aware of the damage.

Level	Attribute Bonus	Body Cost	Price
1	+1 Quickness, +1 Strength, +1 Willpower, +2 Reaction	1.25	60,000¥
2	+2 Quickness, +2 Strength, +2 Willpower, +4 Reaction	2.50	100,000¥

>>>>>[Be careful, chummers. Anything that gets you worked up will trigger it—anything.]<<<<<
    —Feral <10:03:12/12-07-52>

>>>>>[You dog you.]<<<<<
    —Derric <12:13:26/12-07-52>

>>>>>[MAO can be used to partially suppress the effects of unwanted pump activation. Check it out.]<<<<<
    —The Smiling Bandit <Strikes again!/Ha-Ha-Ha>

ORDER HERE

RATINGS

Legality Rating: **6P-BB**

Availability: **8/12 days**

Street Index: **2.5**

SUPRATHYROID GLAND

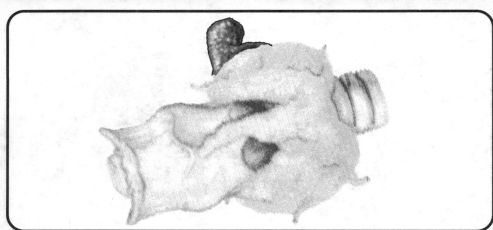

The suprathyroid gland is a regulating gland that is grown, then implanted on top of the thyroid gland in the body. This suprathyroid gland supersedes the metabolic functions of the thyroid, optimizing catabolism (the breakdown of complex substances, such as starches into sugars) and anabolism (the chemical conversion of substances, such as the construction of complex sugars) within the body. The altered metabolism produces more energy and effectively supercharges the recipient. Having a suprathyroid increases all the subject's physical attributes and Reaction by +1. (Quickness raised in this fashion can also increase Reaction.)

The benefits come at a price, however. Individuals implanted with a suprathyroid gland must ingest twice as much food and beverage as the normal person to fuel the higher metabolic rate. If the subject also has symbiotes, the increased food requirements are cumulative. A character who has both a suprathyroid and Level 3 symbiotes, for example, would have to consume four times as much food and beverage as a "normal" person of his/her same race, sex, and age. Because stomach capacity remains the same, this involves either eating twice as often or else purchasing and consuming an expensive (triple normal food costs) diet of tailored nutrients. If a character with both a suprathyroid and symbiotes opts for the tailored diet, his total calculated food requirement is halved. That is, someone with the suprathyroid and the symbiotes-3 would have to eat and drink only twice as much as normal if he were living on the tailored nutrients. As most reactions within the body are exothermic (giving out heat), a person with a suprathyroid gives off more heat, which permits observers with thermographic capability a −1 target modifier to notice him or her. With the higher levels of energy available, characters with a suprathyroid have a tendency toward hyperactivity.

The Reaction bonus has no effect on rigging or decking.

Attribute Bonus	Body Cost	Price
+1 Body, +1 Quickness, +1 Strength, +1 Reaction	1.4	50,000¥

>>>>>[Tendency, my eye. They *are* hyper.]<<<<<
—Neon Samurai <19:34:28/12-07-52>

>>>>>[HYpEracTiVe?! hEy! WHo ArE yoU çAlLinG hYpeRActIVe?]<<<<<
—ScREaMeR <21:32:14/12-07-52>

>>>>>[I rest my case.]<<<<<
—Neon Samurai <23:41:20/12-07-52>

TOXIN EXTRACTOR

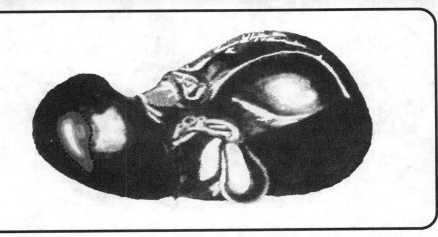

ORDER HERE

RATINGS

Legality Rating: **Legal**

Availability: **4/4 days**

Street Index: **1**

As the main site of catabolism, or the breakdown of complex substances, in the body, the liver is the prime site of defense against potentially toxic compounds and drugs. The toxin extractor is a specially cultivated cluster of cells implanted in the liver to greatly improve the efficiency and to expand the spectrum of catabolic activity. Potential toxins that make their way into the bloodstream are filtered out in the liver, and, with the aid of the extractor, are broken down into harmless fragments and then expelled. A subject with an extractor can reduce the Power Level of a blood-borne toxin attack by 1 point for every two levels of extractor in the body. For example, in a 5D2 blood-toxin attack, a character with a Level 4 toxin extractor would resist against a 3D2 Damage Code.

The maximum level of toxin extractor that can be implanted is equal to the character's unaugmented Body Attribute.

Body Cost   **Price**
.2/level   24,000¥/level

>>>>>[I used to be an alcoholic with massive liver damage. My doctor told me that drinking was going to kill me, so I went out and got myself one of these babies. Now, I'm still an alcoholic, but all I get out of it is the taste.]<<<<<
    —The Man <08:56:114/12-08-52>

>>>>>[Pretty expensive solution for just filtering out alcohol. Why not just drink dealcoholized beverages? Much cheaper. Same effect.]<<<<<
    —Nightfire <10:10:41/12-08-52>

>>>>>[Yeuch!]<<<<<
    —The Man <12:31:26/12-08-52>

ORDER HERE

RATINGS

Legality Rating: **Legal**

Availability: **4/4 days**

Street Index: **1.5**

PATHOGENIC DEFENSE

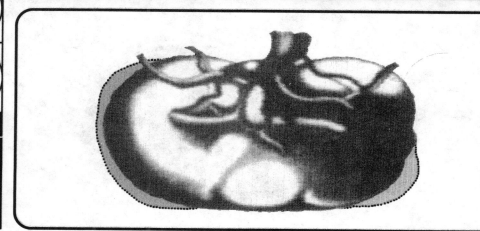

The pathogenic defense augmentation involves an enhancement of the spleen, spearheading the production of more effective and aggressive leukocytes, or white blood cells. These cells are then released into the bloodstream and lymphatic system to combat disease and infection. When combating disease, allergens, microbiologicals, and other foreign particles (not including chemical compounds), reduce the Power Level of the attack by 1 for every 2 levels of pathogenic defense before making the character's Resistance Test. That is, against a 6D2 microbiological attack, a subject with Level 4 pathogenic defense would resist against a 2D2 Damage Code.

The maximum level of pathogenic defense that can be implanted is equal to the character's unaugmented Body Attribute.

Body Cost	Price
.2/level	24,000¥

>>>>>[I understand that my colleagues at Genecraft did an excellent job in the design of this bioware unit. Any comments?]<<<<<
　　—KAM <12:47:52/12-08-52>

>>>>>[Just don't get one of the earlier models. Those buggers attacked and destroyed microbiologicals, but they couldn't differentiate between helpful and harmful microorganisms—they just killed everything. I couldn't digest anything I ate until they fixed that bug. The newer model work great.]<<<<<
　　—Digger <14:27:33/12-08-52>

>>>>>[Hey, KAM, I hear the reason you like this "bioware unit" is that yours saved your hide big-time just recently.]<<<<<
　　—Watching Eye <14:51:59/12-08-52>

>>>>>[No comment.]<<<<<
　　—KAM <16:17:31/12-08-52>

CEREBRAL BOOSTER

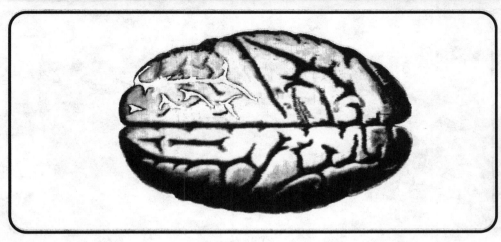

ORDER HERE

RATINGS

Legality Rating: **Legal**

Availability: **6/14 days**

Street Index: **2**

Boosting the brain via a cerebral booster involves the introduction of additional nervous tissue, along with convolutions and gyri (ridges and furrows), into the frontal lobes of the cerebrum. The extra cells and increased surface area improve the efficiency of cognitive and other higher-level functions because the brain areas augmented are those responsible for these functions. Subjects with a Level 1 booster gain +1 to their Intelligence Attribute; a Level 2 booster adds +2 to the recipient's Intelligence. The Intelligence bonus from a Level 1 booster is not cumulative with that given by a Level 2 booster, however. The more advanced booster-2 has the additional advantage of a Task Pool. The levels of a Task Pool can temporarily add dice to a success test. (If a subject has a Task Pool of 1, for example, he may temporarily raise a skill level by +1 for a single test.) The Task Pool refreshes along with the other pools. Technical, Knowledge, and B/R skills are the only skills that can be modified by the Task Pool. The ability to process data on a higher level inherently decreases Reaction time; Intelligence raised in this manner can also increase the Reaction attribute.

Level	Attribute Bonus	Task Pool	Body Cost	Price
1	+1 Intelligence	—	.4	50,000¥
2	+2 Intelligence	1	.8	110,000¥

>>>>>[When one of my mage friends heard about this booster, he went right out and got one installed. Hammerhil said it made him one of the fastest boys in astral space. Don't know if that's true. Ain't never been there myself.]<<<<<
—Tsunami <17:52:03/12-08-52>

>>>>>[Hammerhil? Hey, I remember him. Whatever happened to the old Hammer?]<<<<<
—Winger <18:14:21/12-08-52>

>>>>>[Charbroiled himself with a too-nasty fireball.]<<<<<
—Tsunami <21:46:39/12-08-52>

>>>>>[Guess it didn't make him too smart.]<<<<<
—Ludwig the Mad <23:15:52/12-08-52>

ORDER HERE

RATINGS

Legality Rating: **6P-BA**
Availability: **6-10-12/6 days**
Street Index: **2.5**

DAMAGE COMPENSATOR

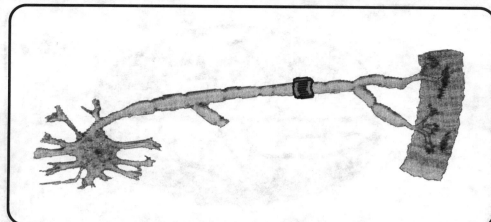

The implanted ribbons of transmissive nerve fiber that form the compensator bypass the safety-inhibitors that would normally prevent individuals from functioning while injured. Damage compensators allow their host bodies to act while suffering from physical and/or mental trauma. Compensators do not block the actual damage, only the neurological and physiological effects of shock and fatigue on the body. As long as physical or mental damage remain equal to or below the compensator's level, the character will not suffer any of the penalties to target numbers or Initiative that usually accompany damage. For example, a character with a Level 3 damage compensator would take no Initiative or target number penalties from damage if both his Physical and Mental Condition Monitors stay equal to or below a Moderate wound. Once either type of damage exceeds the level of the damage compensator, the character will suffer the full effects of the damage; the nervous signals will have become too intense to bypass. Physical and mental damage effects are treated separately for the purposes of calculating compensator action. (If physical damage exceeds the compensator's level but mental damage remains below the compensator's level, the compensator will continue to block the effects of mental damage, but the character will begin to take the regular Initiative and target number penalties from sustaining physical damage.)

The gamemaster may wish to track the damage taken by a player character with a damage compensator, letting the player know that a hit has occurred, but not the severity. A Perception (6) or Biotech (2) Test could reveal the Damage Level of the hit (Light, Moderate, or Serious.)

Level	Availability	Body Cost	Price
1–2	6/6 days	.2/level	25,000¥/level
3–5	10/6 days	.2/level	50,000¥/level
6–9	12/6 days	.2/level	100,000¥/level

>>>>>[These compensators can be real life-savers, but you gotta be careful not to get too cocky. Compensators can get loaded up pretty quickly in a firefight. Know when to bug out, chummers. Otherwise you might be fighting one minute and down writhing in shock the next. A compensator gives you a margin. Use it wisely.]<<<<<
—Hatchetman <09:11:44/12-09-52>

>>>>>[Friend o' mine's been having problems running an adrenal pump with a damage-compensator implant. The pump doesn't want to engage. It apparently doesn't think there's a need to.]<<<<<
—Wart <09:14:37/12-09-52>

MNEMONIC ENHANCER

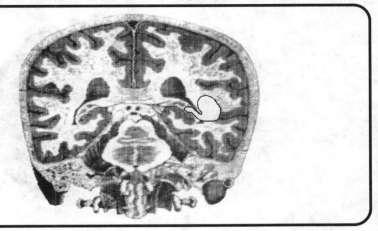

ORDER HERE

RATINGS

Legality Rating: **Legal**

Availability: **6/7 days**

Street Index: **1**

By attaching a highly concentrated growth of gray matter to the hippocampus region of the brain, the mnemonic enhancer can increase the capacity for both short- and long-term memory. A person with a mnemonic enhancer is less likely to forget events or information that he/she encounters. For an Intelligence Test needed to recall a specific event or piece of information, the implanted character receives a +1 die for each level of enhancement. In addition, the increased retention of data facilitates the rapid comprehension of knowledge and language skills; apply a +1 die for every two levels of enhancement to the Target Numbers needed for Knowledge and Language Success Tests.

The maximum level of mnemonic enhancer that can be implanted is equal to a character's unaugmented Body Rating.

To remember something, the character must first have seen or experienced it. In general, the more specific the detail, the more difficult it is to recall. For example, to remember that a car was involved in an accident, the Target Number is 2; it is 3 to remember that the car was red, a 4 to remember the model, a 5 to recall that the driver was male, an 8 to remember seeing the long scratch on the side, and so on—assuming that the character noticed the detail in the first place.

Elapsed time is also an important factor in how difficult or easy it is to remember a particular fact. Apply −1 to the Target Number if the event occurred within the past hour, +0 if within 24 hours, +1 for one week or less, +2 if within the month, +3 if within three months, +4 within four months, +5 within eight months, and so on.

Complexity of the item may also affect the Target Number. A single word with great personal significance might subtract −3 from the Target Number, while a complex passage from a poem once memorized in high school may be +4 or greater.

Body Cost	**Price**
.2/level	15,000¥/level

>>>>>[Drek! I was going to say something about these memory things, but I forget what it was.]<<<<<
—Derric <11:26:19/12-09-52>

>>>>>[Yup, that's why I hang around these places…the humor.]<<<<<
—Fastjack <12:08:41/12-09-52>

ORDER HERE

RATINGS

Legality Rating: **6P-BA**

Availability: **6/6 days**

Street Index: **1.2**

PAIN EDITOR

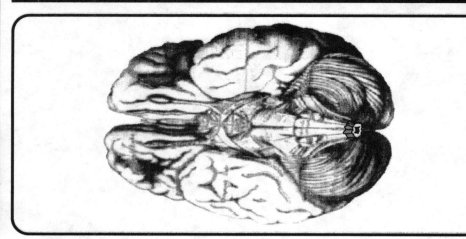

A pain editor is a cluster of specialized nervous tissue designed to filter out specific sensory stimuli. Activation and deactivation of the editor is a learned reflex. When the editor is voluntarily triggered, the individual is no longer subject to any sensations of pain, including feedback pain. With the pain editor active, neither mental damage nor fatigue can render the character unconscious.

Because the character can no longer perceive pain, the gamemaster marks off both physical and mental damage inflicted on the character, but does it out of the player's sight. Note that the character is unaware even of attacks that hit (bullet wounds, a knife stab, and so on), unless he can perceive them in ways other than by pain or tactile sensation. He might, for example, see the weapon hit, note a big spreading spot of red on his white shirt, and so forth. Initiative and target number penalties accompanying mental damage are ignored; penalties resulting from physical damage are applied, but without the player's knowledge (the modifiers would give away the current damage condition). Until the pain editor is actively disengaged, the character (and player) will have no idea of his current damage status. Until he collapses, that is.

Damage is taken and calculated normally. The only difference is that the character remains unaware of the pain involved in being wounded or fatigued. The effects of any sustained damage (initiative and target number penalties or unconsciousness) are applied when the pain editor is "switched off." In addition to the pain-blocking feature, the subject gains a +1 to Willpower when the editor is activated, but suffers a −1 Intelligence loss for the duration. Because the editor works by filtering specific sensory stimuli, a slight deterioration in the tactile sensitivity range also occurs. While the editor is engaged, the subject suffers a +4 to all Target Numbers for tactile-based Perception Tests.

Attribute Bonus	Body Cost	Price
+1 Willpower, −1 Intelligence	.6	60,000¥

>>>>>[Well, chummers, this is probably the most dangerous "augmentation" I have ever seen. You can be dead and not even know it.]<<<<<
—The Smiling Bandit <Strikes again!/Ha-Ha-Ha>

>>>>>[Turning off the body's natural survival monitor is a particularly unwise decision.]<<<<<
—KAM <13:04:17/12-09-52>

>>>>>[During a thrasher one night, I kicked in my editor and didn't sense drek during the entire fight. Not even the sticker in my rib cage. Everything just went black, snap-snap. Next thing I spies is a smiling doc tellin' me how lucky I was not to have gushed to death.]<<<<<
—Tango <17:11:40/12-09-052>

REFLEX RECORDER

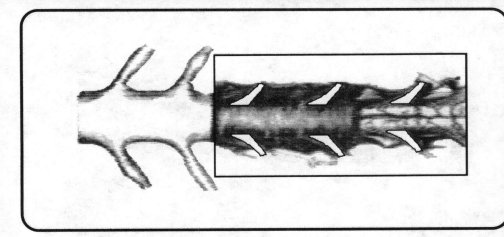

ORDER HERE

RATINGS

Legality Rating: **Legal**
Availability: **5-8/6 days**
Street Index: **1.5**

With this enhancement, extra neural material is deposited and grown in small clusters around each of the 31 pairs of spinal nerves along the spinal cord. These clusters allow "memorization" of certain "learned" motor reflexes, and facilitates their execution. Each recorder allows a character to "learn" one Active or Vehicle Skill (excluding B/R skills) at a +1 die to all future Success Tests. Barring extreme circumstances such as surgical reprogramming, the reflex skill, once learned, cannot be changed; that is, each reflex recorder modifies only a single, pre-chosen skill. The modifier is "permanent," and is applied automatically from that moment on whenever the skill is used.

Recorders can be constructed in two sizes, thus enabling two levels of "memorization." Large masses are used to augment General Skills (Firearms, Athletics, and so on), while the smaller masses are associated with enhancing skill Concentrations (Pistols, Jumping, and the like). Reflex recorders are not cumulative, and cannot be "stacked" to gain more than a single modifier to any single skill. More than one, however, can be implanted to gain similar benefits for multiple skills. Skillwire systems are not compatible with reflex recorders, and so recorders cannot be used to modify any skills acquired through the use of skillwires or skill hardwires.

Type	Availability	Body Cost	Price
Concentration	5/6 days	.1/recorder	10,000¥/ recorder
General	8/6 days	.25/recorder	25,000¥/recorder

>>>>>[Great for repetitive tasks like sighting targets and pulling the trigger.]<<<<<
—Feral <18:04:31/12-09-52>

>>>>>[Or pulling back your fist and slammin' somebody's face over and over.]<<<<<
—Animal <19:39:26/12-09-52>

>>>>>[Don't forget slammin' a head into the pavement a coupla dozen times.]<<<<<
—Bull <20:04:43/12-09-52>

>>>>>[I suppose we can hope you're talking about your own...]<<<<<
—Nightfire <21:09:12/12-09-52>

>>>>>[I've seen a few ambushes really trashed by an overly reflexive trigger finger. Used to know a merc with a recorder and a problem with jumping the gun. Eventually, it got him geeked.]<<<<<
—Hatchetman <22:17:51/12-09-52>

ORDER HERE

RATINGS

Legality Rating: **5P-BB**

Availability: **6/12 days**

Street Index: **2**

SYNAPTIC ACCELERATOR

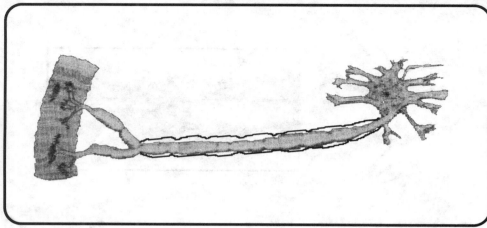

With the implantation of a synaptic accelerator, the neural cells, which make up the spinal cord and other main nerve trunks, are encouraged to replicate and lengthen. This provides a wider "data-path" for the transmission of impulses, and decreases the amount of time required for the signal to traverse the distance. Thus, more data can be sent from and received by the brain in a shorter period of time. Each level of synaptic accelerator adds a cumulative +1D6 to the recipient's Initiative. The synaptic acceleration process is incompatible with boosted or wired reflexes, and cannot be combined with either to produce greater effects.

This Initiative bonus does not assist in rigging or decking.

Level	Initiative	Body Cost	Price
1	+1D6	.3	75,000¥
2	+2D6	1.6	200,000¥

>>>>>[The ultimate in subtle reflex-boosting, but dead last in the performance category.]<<<<<
—Fastjack <06:14:12/12-10-52>

>>>>>[Hey! Sometimes you need the subtlety. Ever tried to sneak wired reflexes past airport security?]<<<<<
—Red Guard <10-27:12/12-10-52>

>>>>>[That, I can safely say, is.something I will never have to worry about.]<<<<<
—Fastjack <11:09:18/12-10-52>

TRAUMA DAMPER

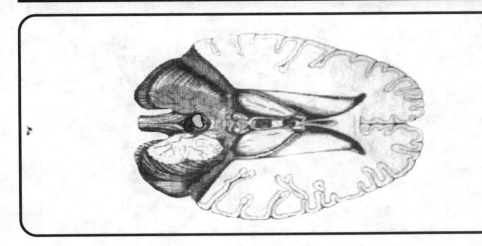

A damper is a clump of specialized receptors, implanted at the base of the thalamus, near the midbrain. Upon receiving sensory information indicating fatigue, pain, or physical trauma, the damper triggers the release of concentrated endorphins and enkephalins (naturally produced opiates and painkillers). This may not remove or aid in the repair of physical damage, but at times it may keep the character alive or conscious enough to deal directly with the cause of the inflicted damage. If the damage (per wound) is physical, shift one box of the indicated Damage Level from Physical to Mental; if the trauma stems from a mental cause, subtract one box from the indicated damage. A trauma damper adds +2 to the target numbers for tasks that cause pain to the character (e.g., interrogation by torture), or it applies a –2 modifier to the target numbers needed to resist pain (e.g., Body or Willpower Tests versus the symptoms of a painful disease).

Because of the feedback-driven nature of the trauma damper, it cannot function properly when used in conjunction with an activated pain editor, and, under certain conditions, a damage compensator. In characters implanted with a damage compensator, the trauma damper will operate properly only when the compensator's ability to handle both Physical and Mental Damage has been exceeded (i.e., when the compensator fails because of excessive damage).

Body Cost	Price
.4	40,000¥

>>>>>[Now *this* is a must-buy for anyone who expects to get into a fight even once in his life. Finest piece of work I ever had installed.]<<<<<
    —Feral <11:38:41/12-10-52>

>>>>>[Thank you for the compliment. I had a few problems implementing the designs, but all in all I'm quite pleased with it myself.]<<<<<
    —KAM <12:56:02/12-10-52>

>>>>>[Don't mention it. Kudos to you for making it. Saved my butt more than once.]<<<<<
    —Feral <13:14:27/12-10-52>

>>>>>[It may help keep you alive, but in certain instances it actually degrades your performance. Like most things, it's a tradeoff.]<<<<<
    —Hatchetman <14:02:12/12-10-52>

ORDER HERE

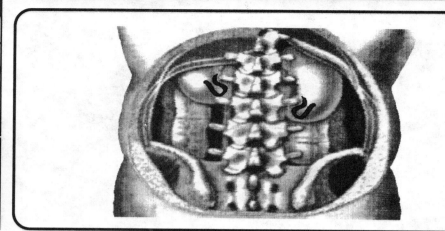

RATINGS

Legality Rating: **Legal**

Availability: **4/4 days**

·Street Index: **1**

NEPHRITIC SCREEN

   With the installation of a nephritic screen, the kidney is rebuilt to enable a more effective cycle of filtration and reclamation. Finer discrimination in the removal of waste products and the reclamation of useful materials extends a greater level of well-being to the recipient. Characters possessing a nephritic screen add +1 to their Body Attribute for tests to resist toxins and pathogenic agents. In addition, the screen acts to combat the effects of pathogens and blood-vectored toxins. Reduce the attack's Power Level by 1 point.

Body Cost	Price
.4	20,000¥

>>>>>[This reminds me: never stiff a street doc.]<<<<<
   —Rapid Fire <13:53:24/12-10-52>

>>>>>[Huh?]<<<<<
   —Spot <14:38:18/12-10-52>

>>>>>[Friend of mine once stiffed a street doc for 50K, then decided to go to another one to get some bioware installed. Turns out Doc B knew Doc A. My, but Bullet was one unhappy term.]<<<<<
   —Rapid Fire <15:20:41/12-10-52>

>>>>>[What happened?]<<<<<
   —Spot <15:58:12/12-10-52>

>>>>>[Doc B turned the screen up to super-fast mode. Does the phrase "bladder-buster" mean anything to you? Twenty minutes between dashes. Never stiff a street doc.]<<<<<
   —Rapid Fire <18:07:19/12-10-52>

EXTENDED VOLUME

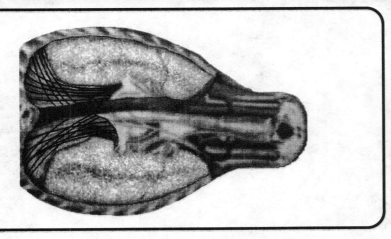

ORDER HERE

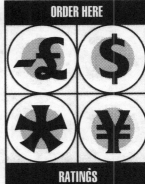

RATINGS

Legality Rating: **Legal**

Availability: **4/4 days**

Street Index: **1**

Although the volume of the air contained in the lungs of an average adult is approximately 2.5 liters, the actual tidal volume (the amount of air that enters and leaves the lungs with each breath), is only .5 liters. By augmenting the amount of flex in the diaphragm, it is possible to increase the tidal volume, thus increasing the efficiency of gas-exchange and, as a result, enhancing stamina. An average adult can hold his breath for approximately 45 seconds; each level of extended volume increases the amount of time a person can hold his breath by an additional 45 seconds. Individuals with extended volume augmentation may also apply modifiers to target numbers in tests of stamina (based on the particular rating of the system enhancement).

Level	Breath	Modifier	Body Cost	Price
1	+45 seconds	−1	.2	8,000¥
2	+90 seconds	−1	.3	15,000¥
3	+135 seconds	−2	.4	25,000¥

>>>>>[Oh, boy. Bigger breaths. Wow. What am I going to do with that?]<<<<<
　　—Wolfman <08:11:32/12-11-52>

>>>>>[How about using it to apply some of that wolfoid halitosis before you use your guns? You know: huff and puff, then blow them all down.]<<<<<
　　—The Smiling Bandit <Strikes again!/Ha-Ha-Ha>

>>>>>[Hardy-har-har.]<<<<<
　　—Wolfman <12:40:26/12-11-52>

ORDER HERE

RATINGS

Legality Rating: **5-BB**

Availability: **10/4 days**

Street Index: **3**

TOXIN EXHALER

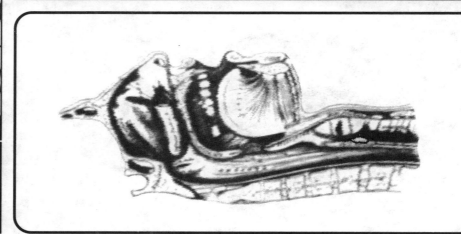

A toxin exhaler is a sac lined with specialized and genetically tailored cells that is implanted in the neck above the larynx (voice box). The cells that line the sac are gengineered to produce a single specific toxin of the recipient's choice. The toxin is stored in the sac until the character wishes to expel the toxin outward. The toxin is expelled by triggering "learned" reflexes; essentially, a massive contraction of the diaphragm, followed by an immediate relaxation, causes a sudden deep breath, followed by a strong exhaling action. The sphincters, which normally keep the sac closed, open slightly during the exhalation, and the resulting effect is much like an aerosol. In average atmospheric conditions (an open area with little or no wind), the cone of effect is similar to an equilateral triangle measuring two meters on each side.

The sac can manufacture only one type of toxin, the one the recipient chooses prior to implantation. Except for removal and replacement of the sac, the toxin cannot be changed or altered once implanted. To prevent accidental injury from the internalized toxin, the character is also partially "immunized" against the toxin. If exposed to the same specific toxin (even if it comes from other sources), the character receives double his "natural" Body Rating (no augmentation) to resist.

The character makes a Quickness (4) Test to hit an intended target. Add +1 to the Target Number per one-half meter to the target. Maximum range equals one-half the unaugmented Body Attribute of the implanted character (round down) in meters.

Body Cost	Price
.6	30,000¥ + (100 times cost of 1 dose of toxin)

>>>>>[Oh, speaking of a bad case of dog-breath…]<<<<<
—Feral <12:54:17/12-11-52>

>>>>>[Now, don't start. You ain't one to talk.]<<<<<
—Wolfman <13:34:25/12-11-52>

>>>>>[This ain't a very practical mode of attack. You have to get in real close to deploy the toxin, which is what's going to happen in most situations. What this exhaler is really meant to be is either a last-ditch defense or a shock (as in surprise) attack. Not many people are going to expect you to breathe them to death—at least not unless you're the Wolfman.]<<<<<
—The Smiling Bandit <Strikes again!/Ha-Ha-Ha>

>>>>>[O.K., that's it. You die.]<<<<<
—Wolfman <16:05:43/12-11-52>

TRACHEAL FILTER

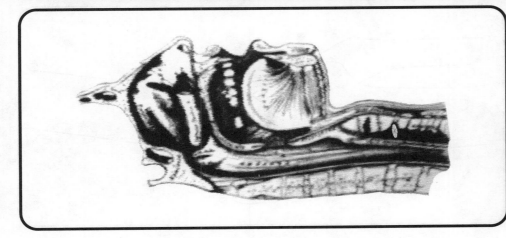

RATINGS

Legality Rating: **Legal**

Availability: **4/4 days**

Street Index: **1**

Traps and filters are implanted at the top of the trachea just below the larynx (voice box). This cluster of specialized tissue absorbs airborne impurities and keeps them from reaching and subsequently affecting the lungs. Solid matter (smoke, pollen, dust, and so on) is easily blocked and expelled with outgoing breath. Gaseous compounds are rendered inert or less effective through the various chemical reactions performed by the filters. Though breathing becomes difficult, the subject will suffer fewer ill-effects (unless the gas itself is inert). Impurities of bacterial size and smaller are not affected by tracheal filters. Each level of filter acts to resist nonmicrobiological air-vectored attacks. Reduce the Power Level of such an attack by one-half the level of the filter (round down) of the character making the Resistance Test. That is, against a 5S2 gaseous attack, an individual with a Level 3 tracheal filter resists against a 2S2 Damage Code.

Body Cost	Price
.2/level	30,000¥/level

>>>>>[I wonder if this will protect me from the Wolfman's breath?]<<<<<
 —The Smiling Bandit <Strikes again!/Ha-Ha-Ha>

>>>>>[Slow and painful, Bandit. Slow and painful.]<<<<<
 —Wolfman <18:21:07/12-11-52>

>>>>>[Just as long as you don't breathe on me—anything but that! Hey! Maybe you should try some of those new Better Breath treats! I hear they clean the teeth while freshening the breath.]<<<<<
 —The Smiling Bandit <Strikes again!/Ha-Ha-Ha>

>>>>>[Dead men leave no time/date stamps.]<<<<<
 —Wolfman <21:13:12/12-11-52>

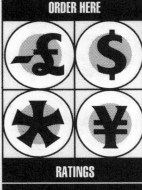

ORDER HERE

RATINGS

Legality Rating: **Legal**

Availability: **5/6 days**

Street Index: **1.5**

ENHANCED ARTICULATION

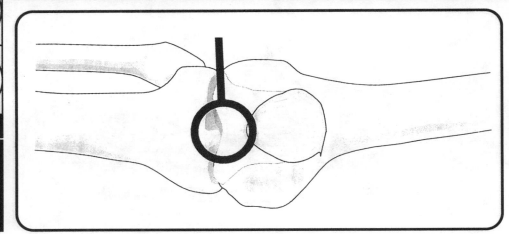

Enhanced articulation is a combination of a number of extensive procedures, including joint-surface coating, relubrication, and tendon/ligament augmentation; these procedures result in a muscle and joint system of extreme fluidity. Enhanced articulation allows a character to execute motion-intensive skills (Active Skills) in a more precise and speedier fashion. Possessors of enhanced articulation roll an additional die when making any Success Test involving an Active Skill. (An individual with Athletics 4 and enhanced articulation, for example, rolls 5 dice when making an Athletics Success Test.) Enhanced articulation also adds a +1 to the Reaction Attribute. Studies show that individuals with enhanced articulation may be immune to many arthritic conditions as a long-term side effect of augmentation.

The Reaction bonus given by the augmentation has no effect on rigging or pure cybernetic decking.

Attribute Bonus	Body Cost	Price
+1 Reaction	.6	40,000¥

>>>>>[A friend of mine just had this procedure done. Let me tell you, the way she can move now is nothing short of phenomenal.]<<<<<
 —Winger <23:31:18/12-11-52>

>>>>>[Awesome is more like it. I've never seen such fluidity in action, at least not in anything human. Makes me want to go out and get it done myself.]<<<<<
 —Neon Samurai <23:56:37/12-11-52>

>>>>>[Are you guys talking about that dancer over at Brigands' again?]<<<<<
 —Ludwig the Mad <00:10:23/12-12-52>

>>>>>[Not even close. And you better hope Evangeline never hears you made the comparison.]<<<<<
 —Winger <00:23:01/12-12-52>

MUSCLE AUGMENTATION

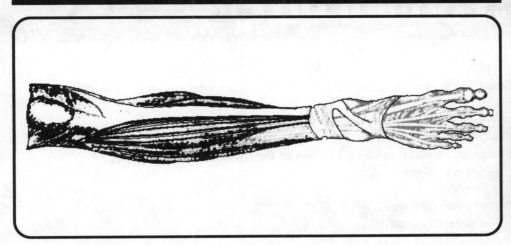

ORDER HERE

RATINGS

Legality Rating: **4P-BC/D**

Availability: **6/6 days**

Street Index: **.9**

The process of muscle replacement has been slowly evolving toward the procedure now known as muscle augmentation. With the development and improvement of biosurgical techniques, the actual removal and replacement of the natural muscle becomes obsolete and unnecessary. Using a biological weaving treatment, an air-injected fluorinated polymer (Teflon™) known as Gortex™ is braided into existing muscle fibers. Gortex, which is chemically inert, is more than four times as strong as natural muscles and ligaments, and, when braided into cables and incorporated into existing tissues, it can increase muscular system performance enormously. Muscles may be enhanced in this fashion to a maximum Level 4 augmentation.

Quickness acquired through muscle augmentation can increase the calculated Reaction Rating.

Bonuses accrued through muscle augmentation do not affect rigging or decking except as they help the character lift bigger engines or carry heavier decks.

Attribute Bonus	Body Cost	Price
+1 Quickness, +1 Strength/level	.8/level	45,000¥/level

>>>>>[I know I can still get muscle replacement, but this stuff is so much more wiz.]<<<<<
—Toymeister <06:37:54/12-12-52>

>>>>>[Not to mention infinitely more Essence-friendly.]<<<<<
—Nightfire <09:50:16/12-12-52>

>>>>>[And infinitely more likely to generate body overstress. And it's much more expensive. Don't forget that.]<<<<<
—Fastjack <10:13:22/12-12-52>

>>>>>[Money's only money. Gadgets are another thing altogether.]<<<<<
—Toymeister <13:48:29/12-12-52>

CYBERTECHNOLOGY

"Gentlemen, we can rebuild him. We have the technology.
Better. Stronger. Faster."
     —Oscar Goldman, "The Six Million Dollar Man"

"Better to be filled with steel than to be filled with lead."
     —Street adage

"Better you than me."
     —Inner-city graffiti

Biotechnology and organic modification are perfect vehicles for optimizing human/metahuman body performance without straying too far from nature's original course. As good as the human body is, it definitely falls short of perfection in terms of design and execution. And no matter how intricate and capable bioware becomes, there will always be many things that the body cannot, and was never intended, to do.

Cybernetics bridges the gap between intent and function. With silicon and steel, man can achieve goals only dreamt of in ages past. Cyberware is not limited by the parameters of flesh. If it can be built, it can be implemented.

Though superior in its performance, cyberware largely fails when it comes to subtlety. The nature of the components themselves makes complete integration into the body difficult. No matter how well-disguised, cybernetic parts will always look somewhat out of place (too smooth in motion, too quick to react, too perfect in appearance, and so on). Though cyberware is cheaper to build and implant than bioware, its inorganic composition and the inherent invasiveness of its integration into the body extract a high price in Essence.

THE MECHANICAL ADVANTAGE

Much of cyberware's ability to out-perform its biological counterparts stems from the fundamental differences in construction material and intention.

The human/metahuman body has evolved with adaptability as its prime concern. It is a multipurpose instrument, able to handle most situations with at least a modicum of ability and therefore a modicum of success. The ingenious design of the human hand, for example, makes it well-suited to handle just about any manipulative task. In contrast, cybernetic prosthetics (and most tools generally) are designed to accomplish specific tasks or functions. Adaptability is sacrificed in favor of designing a device that excels at its designated purpose. A wrench, for example, can turn bolts tighter and loosen stuck bolts with greater ease than a bare hand can, but it is good for little else. At a more basic level, cybernetic components, by their nature and design, can be packed with more performance-boosting hardware than biological systems can afford. For one thing, it is not necessary to design biological life-support processes into

>>>>>[Drek, but cyberware has come a long way since the ole datajack.]<<<<<
     —Reflex <12:07:16/12-12-52>

>>>>>[Yeah, check out those new cranial cyberdecks. Drool.]<<<<<
     —Ludwig the Mad <14:25:38/12-12-52>

>>>[How can anyone expect to keep up? Either money-wise or Essence-wise?]<<<<<
     —Rim Shot <14:42:20/12-12-52>

cybernetic components; additionally, each component is created as a singular, free-standing module. As a result, cybernetic systems can be specifically constructed to get as much performance as physically possible from their component volume.

Added to the benefits inherent in the cybernetic design philosophy is the intrinsic strength of the construction materials themselves. Stronger materials imply higher tolerance factors, greater flexibility, and much more. The inorganic materials of construction, combined with the lack of any direct nervous-system feedback of an internal nature, allow forces to be applied and utilized that would normally cause serious injury to biological components. Most cybernetic prosthetics, for example, have only basic surface-tactile feedback, although more complex nervous arrays are always available.

HUMAN/MACHINE INTERFACE

Because cybernetic augmentation is not limited by the constraints of flesh, it does not face the obstacle of discovering how the brain thinks, perceives, and reacts. It is the job of cyberware to manipulate the brain to think, perceive, and react in the manner that one wishes. That is why the interface between the nervous system and cybernetic implants is the most crucial component of the pairing. Stimuli and information gathered by the prosthetic is passed on to the brain through the interface. Correspondingly, the brain controls the actions of the prosthetic by means of signals that are interpreted through the interface.

Without a well-designed interface, the brain could not readily interpret incoming data. Electrical signals must be converted into impulses that the brain can decode and easily understand—an intricate combination of electrical and chemical commands. Conversely, the interface must also be able to just as easily convert the brain's commands into the language of electronic pulses that drives the machinery of the implanted cybernetics. It is the interface that gives cyberware much of the potential to outperform the human body.

The interface is also the most vulnerable component in any given system. Because so much depends on the proper functioning of the interface, the effects can be dramatic if something goes wrong. Depending on which subsystem is hooked into the unit, the results of a damaged or malfunctioning interface can range from physical paralysis to sensory deprivation and possible neurosis.

Because of the differing natures of cybernetic augmentations, a variety of interface units are necessary for proper cyberware functioning. Each subsystem type must connect to a separate interface module, one for bodyware, one for headware, one for matrixware, and one for senseware. There is no additional cost for such modules.

CYBERNETIC SUBSYSTEMS

The four types of cyberware augmentation are Matrix-oriented, cerebral, sensory, and body-functional. Each subsystem type uses a separate interface, though any bodyware that requires no overt control or cerebral feedback (dermal plating, bone lacing, and so on) does NOT require a link to an interface. Once a particular interface has been installed, all other cyberware of that type can usually channel through that interface. Once a character has cybereyes, for example, he does not need another sensory interface to later install audio cyberware. He simply uses the unit implanted with his cybereyes.

BODYWARE

Bodyware is the most diverse of the four categories, covering everything from dermal armor to wired reflexes. It ranges from enhancements and augmentations to the functional capabilities of the human/metahuman machine. It is bodyware that is most responsible for the colorful and larger-than-life reputation cybernetics has for doing the impossible. Though the stories are largely exaggerated, most are based on solid facts. Cybernetic bodyware does permit one to run faster, leap farther, and take a great deal more punishment. One cannot, however, toss trucks with impunity, outrace a Lamborghini, or land on one's feet from 20 stories up. Not, at least, without expecting to suffer some ill effects.

For bodyware, the weakest link is the frailty of the human/metahuman form. Performance levels could be pushed further, but then the body itself would begin to suffer. Flesh can only be reinforced and strengthened so much before it is no longer flesh.

HEADWARE

Cerebral cyberware focuses mainly on data and calculation. Stressing augmentation over replacement, headware improves system performance by taking over repetitive and heavy computational tasks, leaving the creative processes solely in the

>>>>>[Sure does put the fear of obsolescence in ya, don't it? Heh-heh. "You're obsolete, obsolete, obsolete!"]<<<<<
—The Smiling Bandit <Strikes again!/Ha-Ha-Ha>

>>>>>[And you're dead.]<<<<<
—Wolfman <17:09:51/12-12-52>

>>>>>[You can always trade up, can't you?]<<<<<
—The Man <20:11:41/12-12-52>

domain of the biological. Normal bodies ignore about 90 percent of incoming sensory data, but with subprocessors implanted to handle peripheral functions, the organic brain is free to concentrate on more important matters. In a similar manner, other subprocessors can take over the body's autonomic functions, further liberating the brain's processing time and power for other tasks.

The interface between headware and the brain is the most complex and delicate of such linkages. Integrating the cold, logical calculations with the hot, inspirational flashes is difficult at even the simplest of times. When both systems are working at their peak, information overload becomes a severe problem. When the interface has been calibrated correctly, however, the resulting synergy between man and machine is more than worth the effort.

MATRIXWARE

Internalized equipment designed to work the matrix from a mobile environment is a relatively new advancement in the field of cybernetics. Matrixware puts the decker into the field, while keeping him relatively unobtrusive. Instead of having to lug around a large portable deck, a decker with matrixware components can plug directly into a system. If equipped with the proper equipment, he can run the Net from virtually anywhere.

Matrixware is similar in structure to regular cyberdeck hardware. It is modular, with the individual parts combining to form a working deck. Unlike cyberdecks, the only way to upgrade previously implanted matrixware is to surgically remove and reinstall it. Like cyberdecks, matrixware is quite expensive at the high end.

Damage to matrixware components may occur through both physical trauma and Matrix combat.

SENSEWARE

The superiority of cybernetics over biologicals is most evident in the realm of sensory enhancement. Cybertechnology can readily rebuild any of the organic sensory collectors to include a wider array of sensitivity and function. Not only can existing senses be augmented, but new senses can be added as well. Almost any information-gathering device can be integrated into the human/metahuman sensory system. If it can be hooked into the sensory interface, it can function as a sensory input device.

Nowhere is the power of interface technology better demonstrated than in senseware implants. By interpreting the received sensory information into a form recognized by the brain, senseware allows the individual to observe and participate in worlds previously closed to the human races—the worlds of infrared, ultraviolet, super and subsonics, to name just a few.

>>>>>[You reach a point of diminishing returns. After one upgrade, you start losing more than you gain from trading up. The best course of action is to install the best model straight off the top and only upgrade when you absolutely must. If you can't afford the top-of-the-line unit, try saving up until you can. It's worth it in the long run.]<<<<<
—Sinner Sue <22:20:44/12-12-52>

>>>>>[Only if you're in it for the long run, Sue. Me, I intend to make some fast nuyen now, and then retire. Give it half a chance and this biz'll kill ya.]<<<<<
—Rapid Fire <23:33:47/12-12-52>

>>>>>[Death is just another expression of obsolescence.]<<<<<
—The Smiling Bandit <Strikes again!/Ha-Ha-Ha>

CYBERSYSTEM IMPLEMENTATION

The integration of man and machine occurs on a very intimate and delicate level, one far more subtle than a surgeon with a scalpel could hope to achieve. It's true that a surgeon can position the cyber components within the body, but the job of actually linking the cybernetic device to the human/metahuman nervous system is left to genetically engineered microsurgical units called nanites.

Nanites are small, single-cell organisms that come in many varieties. Two specific types are directly involved in implantation surgery: threaders and coaters. A threader's outer protein shell/wall is impregnated with an inorganic conductive material, usually platinum or gold. The internal metabolism of threaders has been altered to function only on beta-galactose (a sugar derivative that forms only rarely under natural conditions). Through the implantation of a "suicide gene," the threader's metabolism has been additionally altered so that, in consuming the b-galactose, it produces a toxin, which, in time, accumulates within the threader and will eventually kill it.

When an individual is ready for the final stages of cyberware integration, b-galactose is introduced into his bloodstream and guided into the requisite pattern through the use of NMR (nuclear magnetic resonance) devices. Threaders are then injected into the bloodstream. The nanites converge and congregate at the b-galactose sites and eventually die from the self-produced toxins. A simple enzyme treatment then dissolves away the protein shells, leaving a surface-bonded layer of the platinum or gold conductive material that was impregnated within the threader's cell wall. As a final step, coaters are then released into the bloodstream. These nanites are attracted to the conductive material left by the threaders. They will attach themselves to it before dying, leaving a protective protein sheath.

By varying the inorganic material contained in the threader's wall, the NMR-guided pattern of b-galactose laid down, and by repeating the process, it is possible to lay down anything from a simple transmissive fiber to a complex microprocessor. Depending on the complexity of the connections, the entire integration process can take anywhere from one hour to three days, during which the subject must remain more or less motionless. This time is added to the normal recovery period for surgery. (See **Healing Table** and **Elective Surgery**, pages 143 and 144, **Shadowrun**, for details).

At some point, an individual may decide to remove one or more of his cybernetic augmentations. The most common motive is the desire to upgrade the unit. Whatever the reason, removal of such an implant involves a visit to the doctor.

Removing previously implanted cyberware does not bring a return of the Essence spent for that cyberware. Essence, once expended, is gone forever. Under ideal circumstances, the character now has an "open slot" equal to the Essence cost of the removed system. If, for example, a character with an Essence of 3.5 removes a cybereye (0.2 Essence cost), he now has a slot of 0.2 Essence into which additional cyberware can be "installed." That Essence does not return; the character's Essence Rating remains at 3.5. If no new cyberware is installed in that slot, the character's Essence remains at 3.5 forever.

Since the world is not ideal, the character does risk losing extra Essence during the surgery to remove the cyberware. Make a Success Test based on the performing surgeon's Biotech (B/R) or Cybernetics (B/R) Skill, whichever is lower, against a Target Number of 10 minus the patient's current Essence (round down.) If the test generates no successes, the character has lost an additional 10 percent of the Essence cost of the cyberware (round up to the nearest tenth). This lost Essence does not become part of the open slot, but is gone forever. Reduce the character's permanent Essence by the lost amount.

If upgrading, continue with the procedures described on p. 97, **Street Samurai Catalog**. Like bioware, pieces of cyberware such as reflex enhancers, once implanted, cannot be removed without harming the owner. The gamemaster is the final arbitrator on which cyberware is removable in his game.

SYSTEM DAMAGE

Although cybernetic systems can outperform biological systems, they are also more prone to failure through system damage because they lack bioware's intrinsic capacity for self-repair. In the event that any single wound inflicts Serious or Deadly physical damage, check for possible system damage.

If the result was a Serious wound, roll 1D6 and subtract 4; for Deadly wounds, roll 1D6 and subtract 2. The die result indicates the number of potential components that might have been damaged. Having determined this number, learn what specific cyberware is affected by rolling randomly or simply by gamemaster fiat. (See also pp. 93–95 of **Street Samurai Catalog** for more on one method.) Cortex bombs, fingertip compartments, and other such cyberware chosen by the gamemaster

>>>>>[You would know.]<<<<<
    —Wolfman <02:12:51/12-13-52>

>>>>>[I took out one of those Renraku cyberdogs using an interface hit. Dropped the puppy right in its tracks.]<<<<<
    —Trigger Man <07:21:31/12-13-52>

>>>>>[That's, like, maybe a one-in-a-million shot! I would never risk my life trying to shoot for the cyberware. It's far easier to take down the meat than it is to damage the metal.]<<<<<
    —Feral <09:25:08/12-13-52>

cannot be damaged in this fashion, and are not considered when determining possible system damage. If the random roll generates a repeat result, consider it a "No system hit" for that particular roll.

If the die result indicates that at least one system has potentially been affected, there is a 1 in 36 chance that an interface module is among the components affected. To determine whether an interface unit has been damaged, roll 2D6. If the result totals a 2, one of the neural interfaces has been hit. Roll randomly to determine which interface.

Next, roll 1D6 for each affected component to determine the extent of damage:

    0 = No damage
    1–2 = Light
    3–4 = Moderate
    5 = Serious
    6 = Deadly
    7 = Destroyed.

For custom cyberware, alpha or beta grade, make the Damage Resistance Test described on p. 98 of **Street Samurai Catalog**. Each success reduces by 1 the Damage Level given above. None of the cyberware presented in the book is currently available in either alpha or beta grades.

Once a system suffers Light damage, it operates at 50 percent efficiency until repaired or replaced (all bonuses are halved, dropping fractions). For example, a smartgun link with Light damage is only –1 to the Firearms Success Test Target Number, instead of the normal –2. If the damage is Moderate (or later accumulates to the Moderate level), all bonuses, features, and normal operations cease to function. The aforementioned smartgun link would then be at –0 to the Target Numbers, and would stop giving any data to the linked character. At the Serious level, moderate system feedback from accrued component damage begins to impede overall performance. Add +1 to Target Numbers for all rolls the character makes; this penalty is cumulative with all other penalties, including other damaged systems. At the Deadly wound level, system feedback goes wild, severely affecting overall performance; the Target Number penalty increases to +2. This penalty is also cumulative, i.e., two systems at Deadly wound level add +4 to all Target Numbers, in addition to any other penalties normally suffered. If the damage level exceeds Deadly in severity, the component is considered "destroyed," negating all penalties from the unit's adverse system feedback.

Resolve damage to interface units separately. The effects are similar to those in specific system hits, but affect all components connected to the damaged module. That is, if the sensory interface suffers a Light wound, all the senseware augmentations would behave as if suffering a Light wound, including the +1 Target Number penalties for each connected system. However, damage inflicted in this manner is "virtual" damage (as only the interface suffers any real damage). It is not necessary to repair systems affected by damage to the controlling interface, and penalties disappear as soon as the damaged module is repaired or replaced. If a connected system is already at the same damage level or higher, it operates at the higher penalty. For example, if a cybereye with Deadly damage is connected to a senseware interface with Serious damage, the cybereye operates at a +2 penalty rather than a +1.

Repair of cybernetic systems is relatively straightforward. For all tests pertaining to cyberware implantation/removal/repair, use the attending character's Biotech (B/R) or Cybernetics (B/R) Skill, whichever is lower. The Target Number for repairs are 2 for Light damage, 3 for Moderate damage, 4 for Serious damage, and 8 for Deadly damage. A destroyed component may not be repaired, only removed and replaced (with no return of any invested Essence). For repairs of custom cyberware, double the Target Number for alpha grade, and triple it for beta grade systems. Base repair time for Light damage is equal to twice the base (unmodified) Essence cost of the component in hours. For Moderate damage, double the needed time, triple for Serious, and quadruple for Deadly. Each success resulting from the Repair Test reduces the time required. To determine the actual repair time, divide the base repair time by the number of successes. Repairs to cyberware components do not cost additional Essence, and Magic loss is not possible.

Cost for repair parts are determined from the original cost of the component. To calculate cost for parts, multiply the original cost by 0.05 if the damage is Light, 0.1 if Moderate, 0.2 if Serious, and by 0.4 if the damage is Deadly. Labor costs are derived from the attending character's procedural skill. Base labor rates are 50¥ for each skill level per hour, i.e., labor for a three-hour job by a Skill Level 6 cybertechnician would cost 900¥. This rate is further modified by the quality of facilities available and by other market conditions.

In terms of repair, treat interface modules as having an Essence cost of 1, a nuyen cost of 20,000¥, and as being of alpha grade.

>>>>>[What Trigger Man fails to mention is that he was shooting at the pooch with an SMG on full automatic. The interface hit was just a lucky shot. It's impossible to actually aim for the interface. Upon examining the animal to make sure it was going to stay down, I concluded that another shot would have killed the thing anyway. Those are tough dogs.]<<<<<
    —Reflex <11:36:12/12-13-52>

>>>>>[Lucky shot or not, cyberware hits can be pretty horrible. The more chrome you sport, the better the chance you take a system hit one of these days.]<<<<<
    —Neon Samurai <12:41:11/12-13-52>

CYBERWARE

"I'll have one of those, and two of those, and oh yeah! Two! Definitely two of those!"
    —Toymeister, Gadget aficionado

"Sounds wiz…but is it Essence-friendly?"
    —Bolt, Hermetic mage

Cyberware is the ultimate gestalt of man and machine. And if technology is a representative index of the level of a civilization, cybertechnology presents a disturbing picture. It reflects a high level of knowledge and sophistication, harnessed to take mankind to the edge of perfection—and a society that uses this perfection to kill.

With the right cyberware, one could be the fastest, strongest, and the deadliest. All it costs is humanity, and in 2053, that's a fair trade to stay alive.

>>>>>[Fair trade? All I get outta the deal is shots fired at me from out of the shadows, warrants for my arrest in three nations, a leg that gives out under stress, and a shoulder that squeaks when it gets cold.]<<<<<
    —Chrome <13:15:17/12-13-52>

>>>>>[What about those condoplexes south of the border, the two separate Geneva-Orbital cred accounts, and the new Ferrari you just bought? Tough life, chummer. My hydraulics leak for you.]<<<<<
    —Digger <14:02:51/12-13-52>

ORDER HERE

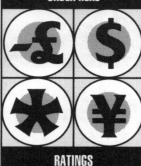

RATINGS

Legality Rating: **6P-CA/ B/C**
Availability: **5/14 days**
Street Index: **1.5**

BONE LACING

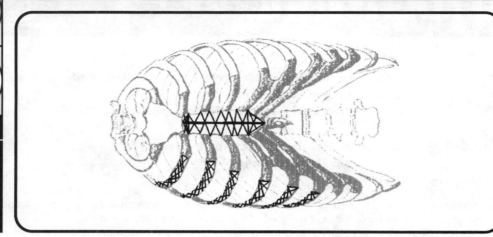

Bone lacing is a lengthy and expensive process in which the cellular structure of the subject's bones is augmented with lattice chains of reinforcing plastics and metals to improve the bone's integrity and tensile strength. There is some weight gain; weight added this way counts toward calculated encumbrance (plastic, +5 kg; aluminum, +10 kg; titanium, +15 kg). Along with plastic derivatives, aluminum and titanium are the only metals that have proved suitable for the procedure to date (with titanium obviously being the more expensive). Plastic or aluminum lacing adds +1 to the character's Body Attribute; titanium adds +2. Aluminum lacing also gives one level of impact armor, while titanium lacing adds one level of impact armor plus an additional level of ballistic protection. Armor gained in this fashion is cumulative with worn armor.

Unarmed blows by persons with plastic bone lacing are at (Str + 1)M2, (St + 2)M2 for aluminum, and (Str + 3)M2 for titanium. Lacing makes bones virtually unbreakable by conventional standards; laced bones can still be broken if a large enough deliberate force is applied. The Barrier Rating for plastic is 6, for aluminum 8, and for titanium it is 10. Aluminum and titanium lacings will show up on conventional metal detectors.

A character with bone lacing can also choose to have his unarmed blows do physical damage, but the Power Level of the attack is halved (round up).

Material	Bonus	Unarmed Blow	Essence Cost	Price
Plastic	+1 Body	(Str + 1)M2	.50	7,500¥
Aluminum	+1 Body, +1 Impact	(Str + 2)M2	1.15	25,000¥
Titanium	+2 Body, +1 Impact, +1 Ballistic	(Str + 3)M2	2.25	75,000¥

>>>>>[Hitting a guy with lacing is only slightly less painful than hitting a wall made out of whatever the guy's laced with.]<<<<<
—Feral <15:15:15/12-13-52>

>>>>>[Yeah, and both examples aren't highly recced. In the latter case, you mangle your fist. In the former, you torque the guy off, then mangle your fist.]<<<<<
—Rapid Fire <16:20:14/12-13-52>

>>>>>[Well, now, that all depends on how hard you intend to hit him. If he breaks first...]<<<<<
—Thor <18:51:48/12-13-52>

HYDRAULIC JACK

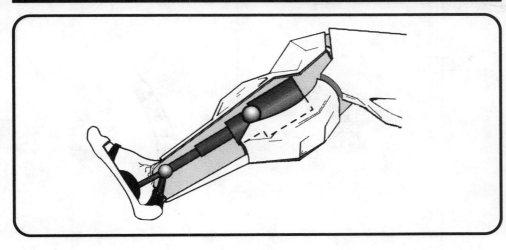

ORDER HERE

RATINGS

Legality Rating: **Legal**

Availability: **5/6 days**

Street Index: **1**

When installed in standard cyberleg replacements, a hydraulic jack dramatically increases leaping capability. A character equipped with a hydraulic jack multiplies his normal maximum leaping distance or height by the jack's level to determine the new limits. A Level 3 hydraulic jack, for example, triples the distances and heights normally achieved. Hydraulic jacks can only be installed in a cyberleg.

If a character can manage to land on his feet, hydraulic jacks can also absorb some of the impact involved in a fall. (Landing on one's feet needs a successful Athletics (5) Test for a height of 5 meters or less, +1 to the Target Number for every additional 4 meters.) Reduce the Power Level of the fall by the jack's level. Landing successfully on his feet after an 8D2 fall, an individual with Level 2 hydraulic jacks only suffers the effects of a 6D2 fall.

Essence Cost	Levels	Price
.25	1–6	5,000¥/level

FALLING

All falls have a damage code of D2, with the Power Level of the fall's "attack" being one-half the number of meters fallen (round down). The character may use body dice in the Damage Resistance Test to reduce the damage. Subtract one-half the character's Impact Armor Rating (round down) directly from the Power Level of the fall. Athletics Skill may be also used. Make an Athletics Skill Test (or appropriate Concentration/Specialization) against a Target Number equal to the number of meters fallen. Subtract each success generated directly from the Power Level of the fall before the Damage Resistance Test. The player cannot make both this test and the Athletics Test for the hydraulic jack: he must choose one or the other.

>>>>>[Ah, the last piece of equipment I need to complete my repertoire. Yep, wired reflexes-3, muscle augmentation-5, and now cyberlegs with a hydraulic jack-6.]<<<<<
　　—Kent <23:08:41/12-13-52>

>>>>>[So what?]<<<<<
　　—Rim Shot <06:12:24/12-14-52>

>>>>>[So now I'm faster than a speeding bullet, more powerful than a locomotive, and able to leap tall buildings in a single bound.]<<<<<
　　—Kent <08:53:48/12-14-52>

>>>>>[What the frag does that mean?]<<<<<
　　—Rim Shot <09:31:14/12-14-52>

ORDER HERE

RATINGS

Legality Rating: **Legal**

Availability: **3/24 hours**

Street Index: **.8**

MEMORY

Advances in computer microtechnology and high-density optical chemistry have made internal memory more "Essence-friendly," with a relatively small increase in its monetary cost. All memory is implemented in a first-in-first-filed (FIFF) architecture that fills all available space to ensure the fullest possible use of existing memory. As data accumulates, however, it takes longer to sift through the memory banks to retrieve requested information. System load delay (SLD) can be calculated using the simple formula: $SLD = MpU/250$ (MpU is the number of megapulses used). System load delay is measured in turns. As internal memory is intrinsically faster than the memory used to produce skillsofts, it is generally recommended that skillsoft users upload them into internal memory to reduce the amount of delay time. Installation of an I/O subprocessor unit can also reduce SLD.

Essence Cost	Price
Mp/300	Mp x 150¥

>>>>>[Finally! It's about time somebody came up with something like this. Maybe now you can get enough memory to do something with.]<<<<<
    —Findler-Man <14:20:54/12-14-52>

>>>>>[If you're having memory problems, check out the Data Management SPU in a few.]<<<<<
    —Toymeister <15:13:00/12-14-52>

DATAJACK

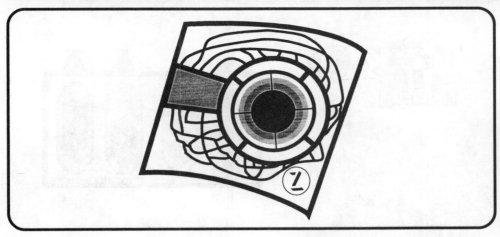

ORDER HERE

RATINGS

Legality Rating: **Legal**

Availability: **Always**

Street Index: **.9**

As cybertechnology and cyberware have grown in sophistication, so has the ubiquitous datajack. An improved datajack can now increase performance levels by increasing the data flow rate (DFR), measured in megapulses per turn. Once a datajack has been installed, the user still needs an Input/Output control device (an encephalon or I/O subprocessor) implanted before he gains full access to all internal memory and headware peripherals. Information can be uploaded, downloaded, and otherwise manipulated at a rate equal to the datajack's DFR. The jack's DFR cannot be boosted by the addition of an I/O subprocessor or by any other means except through a direct datajack upgrade.

The datajack listed in the **Shadowrun** rules has a DFR of 25 and comes with a Level 0 I/O processor SPU.

Level	DFR	Essence Cost	Price
1	25	.10	500¥
2	50	.15	1,000¥
3	75	.20	2,000¥
4	100	.25	4,000¥

>>>>>[Big wiz! A faster datajack, too! Adios, performance problems.]<<<<<
—Findler-Man <15:45:36/12-14-52>

>>>>>[Yup. And up to four times the flow-rate of the old datajack.]<<<<<
—Toymeister <16:01:45/12-14-52>

SOFTLINK

ORDER HERE

RATINGS

Legality Rating: **Legal**

Availability: **3/72 hours**

Street Index: **.9**

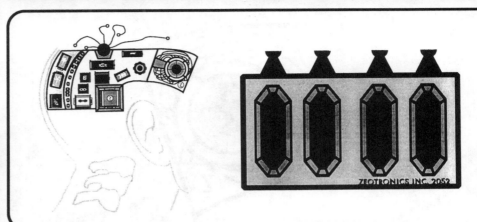

Designed to replace the outdated chipjack, a softlink contains all the necessary hardware for the human brain to interpret and utilize skillsofts and datachips, though using Active skillsofts still requires the installation of skillwire systems. Because the softlink adapter can handle up to four chips in any combination, it is no longer necessary to install more than one port to benefit from the use of multiple skillsofts. Like all systems, however, as the processing load increases, so does the system load delay (SLD). The more megapulses the softlink must process, the slower becomes the response time. Calculate softlink system load delay (SSLD) in turns with the formula: $SSLD = MpL/100$ (MpL is the megapulse load, the total number of Mp of information stored in all the data/skillsofts plugged into the softlink). Because the softlink system is external to all other headware systems, SSLD is separate from headware system delay (i.e., an individual can have two delay numbers, one for his softlink system and one for the rest of his headware). To decrease SSLD requires the addition of an I/O subprocessor unit. If desired, more than one softlink may be implanted.

Level	Ports	Essence Cost	Price
1	1	.15	1,000¥
2	2	.20	2,000¥
3	3	.25	4,000¥
4	4	.30	8,000¥

>>>>>[Now, this is an idea that took its time getting to market.]<<<<<
　　—Ludwig the Mad <16:29:52/12-14-52>

>>>>>[But very much worth the wait. Just think, four skillsofts at a time!]<<<<<
　　—Toymeister <17:08:22/12-14-52>

>>>>>[It's even more impressive when linked up to a skillwire system. Up to four Active skillsofts at a time. You can go from ultra-klutz to Doug Danger/Master of Gong-Fu/Mr. Decathlon/Sureshot McGraw just by slotting some chips.]<<<<<
　　—Reflex <17:24:09/12-14-52>

SKILLWIRE PLUS

The venerable skillwire system has recently been upgraded and enhanced to bring it on par with current technology. Required for the use of Active skillsofts, the skillwire system translates the mnemonic coding on the skillsoft to real-time neurological impulses and thus to physical activity. The total ratings of all the skillsofts in use at any one time may not exceed the Total Ratings capability of the system. Skillsofts, regardless of whether inserted into a chipjack, softlink, or uploaded into headware memory, can only be used at the rating for which they are coded. Use at a reduced rating is not possible.

Skillwire Classic systems, like those listed in the **Shadowrun** rules, can only handle up to their level in total accessible skillsoft ratings.

Level	Essence Cost	Total Ratings	Legality	Availability	Price
1–3	Level x .10	Level x 2	Legal	4/10 days	Level x 15,000¥
4–6	Level x .20	Level x 2	6P–CB	5/10 days	Level x 125,000¥
7–9	Level x .30	Level x 2	4P–CB	12/20 days	Level x 1,000,000¥

>>>>>[Baby! Who needs youth and learning experiences. Pull me from the womb, tabula rasa, let me sleep for eighteen years, then jack me in with big wiz skillsofts with only the finest memories, top'-o-the-line, bang-bang and let me at 'em! Why I could…Hey, wait a minute….]<<<<<
　　　—Big Joe <17:55:41/12-14-52>

>>>>>[Scary thought, *neh*?]<<<<<
　　　—Neon Samurai <18:02:12/12-14-52>

ORDER HERE

RATINGS

Legality Rating: **Legal**
Availability: **Varies/4 days**
Street Index: **1.25**

SKILLSOFT

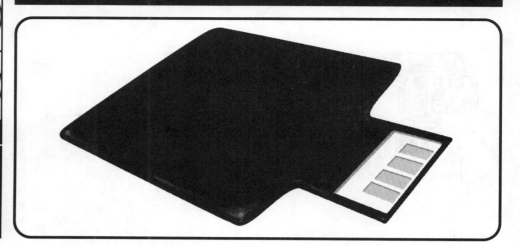

Memories on a chip. When used in conjunction with the proper headware and bodyware, skillsofts allow users to know and do things they never learned themselves. Because a skillsoft's "memory imaging" encoding differs radically from actual memories or learned experiences the user may already have, the skillwire system must override the user's own reflexes, abilities, and memories, forcing him to rely on the encoded capabilities. If a skillsoft duplicates a skill that a character already possesses naturally, only the skillsoft's rating applies. The character loses his natural ability for the duration of the skillsoft access.

Skillsofts come in three types. A *knowsoft* replicates Knowledge Skills like Science or Mental Skills. A subclassification of knowsoft are the *linguasofts,* which allow language use and replicate a Language Skill. A *datasoft* is raw data, pure information like that found in a textbook. No application or comprehension ability comes with the datasoft, just the data. An *activesoft* replicates an Active Skill like Combat, Physical, Technical, or Vehicle Skill.

To access a knowsoft requires a chipjack, softlink, or uploading into memory for access with an encephalon. Datasofts can be accessed through a datajack, chipjack, or softlink to a display or datasoft link or into headware memory and out to a display link or datasoft link/encephalon. Skillwire systems are required for the use of activesofts.

MEMORY REQUIRED
(in Megapulses)

Skill Type	Rating									
	1	2	3	4	5	6	7	8	9	10
General	10	20	30	200	250	300	700	800	900	2,000
Concentration	6	12	18	120	150	180	420	480	540	1,200
Specialization	4	8	12	80	100	120	280	320	360	800
Language	3	6	9	24	30	36	70	80	90	300

SKILLSOFT COSTS

Type	Availability	Cost
Knowsoft	5/4 days	Mp x 150¥
Linguasoft	6/36 hours	Mp x 50¥
Datasoft	4/4 days	Varies with value of data
Activesoft	6/4 days	Mp x 100¥

>>>>>[Word to the wise: when you are in the field, make sure your skillsofts are catalogued and marked properly. It's really unwiz to slot "Advanced Taiwanese Pastry IV" when what you really needed was that Gunnery soft.]<<<<<
　　—Hatchetman <18:08:45/12-14-52>

>>>>>[Voice of experience, perhaps?]<<<<<
　　—The Smiling Bandit <Strikes again!/Ha-Ha-Ha>

ENCEPHALON

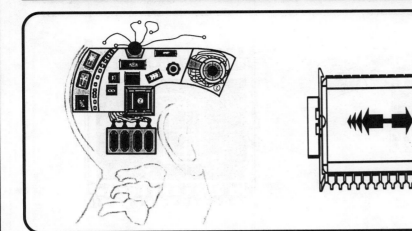

An encephalon is a combination microcomputer and expert system that permits the brain to access all internal memory stores and functions. It operates as both a background processor and an interpreter/host system for skillsoft programs.

The microcomputer uses its processing power to augment the user's own information-processing abilities, providing bonuses to the owner's Intelligence for certain Technical, Knowledge, and B/R Skills (Intelligence raised in this fashion can increase the character's Reaction Rating). Levels from an encephalon's Task Pool may be used as bonuses to the user's skills (temporarily adding to the number of dice rolled for any Skill Test). The Task Pool is refreshed along with all other dice pools.

The encephalon also has a hardwired skillsoft host system similar to that of the softlink system, allowing use of both external and uploaded skillsofts. An encephalon is needed to use uploaded skillsofts. The data contents will be present, but the "naked" brain is unable to comprehend the data in such a raw form.

An encephalon precludes the need for a softlink to make use of datachips or skillsofts. Limits do exist for using the encephalon in this way, however. A character can plug only one datasoft or skillsoft into the datajack at any given time, and the additional data load adds to SLD rather than being considered separately. (To calculate the effect of a datasoft or skillsoft's use in this way, multiply the chip's Mp Rating by 2.5 and add the figure to the MpU.) This being the case, persons who are contemplating heavy use of external skillsofts or datachips are encouraged to purchase a softlink rather than relying purely on the limited abilities of the encephalon to process the load.

Improving the grade and quality of the encephalon will increase processing power, but will not improve upon expert system performance.

Older chipjacks, such as those described in the **Shadowrun** rules, contain early versions of the encephalon. These perform the same functions, but bestow no bonuses. Display links perform the same, non-bonus function as an encephalon for datasofts.

The encephalon does boost magical ability.

Level	Intelligence Bonus	Task Pool	Essence Cost	Price
1	+1 Intelligence	—	.50	15,000¥
2	+1 Intelligence	1 die	.75	40,000¥
3	+2 Intelligence	2 dice	1.50	75,000¥
4	+2 Intelligence	3 dice	1.75	115,000¥

>>>>>[One thing they don't tell you in the owner's manual is that you can use these babies to multitask your cognitive needs.]<<<<<
    —The Smiling Bandit <Strikes again!/Ha-Ha-Ha>

SPU (DATA MANAGEMENT)

ORDER HERE

RATINGS

Legality Rating: **Legal**

Availability: **6/60 hours**

Street Index: **1**

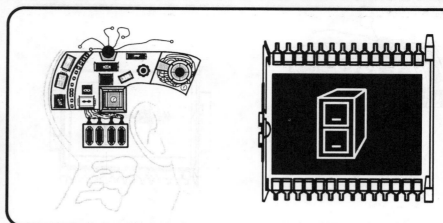

Once a data management subprocessor unit is installed in the cranial interface, it functions transparently to normal functions. That is, no special commands or procedures are necessary to activate the subprocessor. The subprocessor works in conjunction with existing memory, and increases data-storage capacity by using advanced data-compression algorithms. Data to be stored is compressed, and then uncompressed automatically when needed or accessed. While functionally transparent, this SPU shows a more evident and pronounced time lag in system response as the compression ratio increases. The tighter the data is packed, the more time it takes to complete the process. Add the subprocessor's Load Rating to the existing SLD (system load delay, see **Memory,** p. xx). To determine the "actual" amount of memory available for use (and for ease of calculation), increase the existing memory by the subprocessor's Compression Rating. This number becomes the "virtual" memory rating, and represents the system's effective storage capacity. For example, a character with 100 Mp of real memory who also has a Level 3 data management SPU has an effective 175 Mp of storage.

Level	Compression	Load Rating	Essence Cost	Price
1	+25%	—	.10	9,500¥
2	+50%	+1	.15	19,000¥
3	+75%	+1	.20	28,500¥
4	+100%	+2	.25	38,000¥

>>>>>[A great buy—if you don't mind the system delay.]<<<<<
— Findler-Man <18:23:01/12-14-52>

>>>>>[And only if you intend to buy a lot of headware memory.]<<<<<
— Fastjack <20:05:34/12-14-52>

SPU (INPUT/OUTPUT)

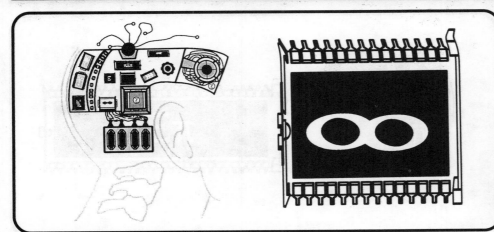

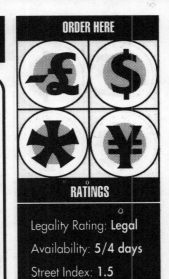

ORDER HERE

RATINGS

Legality Rating: **Legal**

Availability: **5/4 days**

Street Index: **1.5**

Internalized memory is not usable for any purpose by the brain alone. Either an encephalon or an Input/Output subprocessor unit must be integrated into the cranial interface before the brain can access the additional storage capacity.

The I/O subprocessor can be installed without the encephalon, but, on its own, the I/O subprocessor provides only limited access to memory functions—merely the ability to store and recall data. In the case of computer files, the data can be stored and recalled, but cannot be directly accessed. In other words, data stored in this manner is meaningless without an encephalon.

Only when installed in a person who also has an encephalon is the true utility of the I/O subprocessor apparent. Because the encephalon has its own I/O circuitry, the subprocessor can spend its processing power and time speeding up the rate at which data is moved about, drastically cutting the system time tied up in data access. The subprocessor's I/O rating reduces both system load delay (SLD) and softlink system load delay (SSLD). The delay time for a headware system with, say, an SLD 5 drops to SLD 1 with the installation of a Level 3 I/O SPU (the I/O-3 SPU having an I/O Rating of 4).

The Level 0 I/O subprocessor system contained in the datajack listed in the **Shadowrun** rules has an effective I/O rating of 0. See also **Datajack**, above.

Level	I/O Rating	Essence Cost	Price
1	1	.10	5,000¥
2	2	.15	7,500¥
3	4	.20	12,500¥
4	8	.25	22,500¥

>>>>>[Anyone wanting to load up on headware memory or on skillsofts is highly recommended to install an I/O SPU as well.]<<<<<
—Fastjack <20:08:55/12-14-52>

>>>>>[If you're tired of waiting those long seconds for the softlink unit to access your skillsofts, this is the upgrade for you.]<<<<<
—Toymeister <21:39:00/12-14-52>

ORDER HERE

RATINGS

Legality Rating: **Legal**

Availability: **6/60 hours**

Street Index: **1**

SPU (MATH)

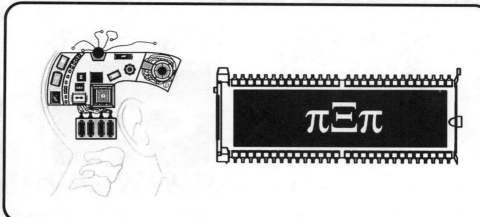

When installed in the user's cranial interface, the math subprocessor can enhance the host's mathematical abilities in two ways. The subprocessor's rating is applied as a bonus to the subject's Mathematics Skill (temporarily adding to the number of dice rolled for any Success Test). The base time to solve a problem is equal to the question's Target Number in seconds—reduced by the number of extra successes. With the subprocessor installed, the character can accomplish all math functions as background tasks, requiring no concentration and, thus, no actions to perform. As a side benefit, the subprocessor also functions as a timepiece, alarm clock, and chronometer, with a second accuracy equal to the square of its rating in decimal places. A Level 3 Math SPU, for example, is accurate up to nine decimal places.

The Math SPU also assists in certain aspects of other skills, such as Technical and Technical (B/R) and Sciences. For those skills, the SPU adds half its level (round down) as a bonus to the skill. Yes, this does mean that it increases the Hacking Pool by one-half its level.

Level	Essence Cost	Price
1	.10	2,000¥
2	.15	5,000¥
3	.20	11,000¥
4	.25	23,000¥

>>>>>[Not a real useful unit all by itself. It becomes a lot more handy in combination with other cybersystems.]<<<<<
—Goosehawk <23:19:32/12-14-52>

>>>>>[I don't think I know any *real* decker who doesn't have a full-blown one of these.]<<<<<
—Findler-Man <23:52:10/12-14-52>

>>>>>[If you say so.]<<<<<
—Fastjack <23:59:59/12-14-52>

TACTICAL COMPUTER

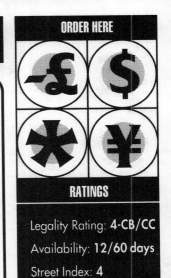

ORDER HERE

RATINGS

Legality Rating: **4-CB/CC**

Availability: **12/60 days**

Street Index: **4**

A tactical computer is a dedicated system designed to keep track of all relevant combat data. If the subject's senses cannot provide the appropriate information, the computer may not be able to make correct decisions. For example, a character without any compensating "vision" ability may be operating in a dark room. Each individual extra sense (low-light, thermographic, hearing amplification, high-frequency, and so on) type present increases the tactical computer's level by 1. The presence of an orientation system (see p. xx) adds 2 to the tactical computer's level.

A tactical computer can keep track of (or "mark") and project the predicted movements of a number of targets equal to its level plus the user's Intelligence Rating. For example, a subject with an Intelligence 4 and a Level 2 tactical computer can mark and predict the motions of up to six targets. To successfully mark a target, the tactical computer must make a Success Test pitting its effective level against a Target Number based on the range to the target as if it were a shotgun. All applicable Ranged Situation Modifiers apply. The extra successes generated should be noted for each target. This is the system's Success Level for each target.

The target can shake the marking by breaking out of the tactical computer's line-of-sight. Doing so forces the tactical computer to attempt to reacquire the target when the target becomes visible again. To do so, roll dice equal to the system's effective level against a base Target Number 1, modified upward by 1 for every meter the target moved while out of line-of-sight and 1 for every full combat turn that has passed. If this test succeeds, the Success Level for that target is now based on the extra successes generated from this test. If the test fails, the target can be re-marked on the character's next Action. The presence of an accurate map of the area (gamemaster's discretion) in headware memory or linked through a datajack reduces the Target Number of the Reacquisition Test by 3 points.

The targeting feature and trajectory computation adds an additional number of dice equal to the previously generated Success Level for that target to all Combat Success Tests against that target. This modifier is applied only to those targets marked by the tactical system, and is valid for both melee and ranged combat.

The computer also has an imbedded tactical expert system. The expert system is used as a bonus to, or in place of, any existing Tactics Skill. This bonus adds to any already present Tactics Skill and does not override the skill rating, as skillwire systems do.

All system functions are background tasks, requiring no Actions to call up or perform. After a failed reacquisition, the computer can attempt a new marking, but only during the user's Action, though it does not cost an Action.

Characters with a tactical computer add the computer's rating to their Initiative. An Initiative value calculated in this fashion cannot exceed the normal Reaction maximum, however. That is, if a subject has a Reaction 4 +1D6 and a Level 2 tactical computer, he may add +2 when determining his Initiative, but can never exceed a total Initiative of 10.

Tactical computer bonuses do not assist in rigging or decking.

Level	Essence Cost	Legality	Price
1	3.5	4-CB	350,000¥
2	4.0	4-CC	900,000¥
3	**CLASSIFIED**	2-CC	**CLASSIFIED**
4	**CLASSIFIED**	1-CC	**CLASSIFIED**

>>>>>[This gives you edge in spades. But try finding one on the market. They're also illegal for civilians to possess in just about all the states in the UCAS and all the territories in North America. Just a minor technicality.]<<<<<
   —The Smiling Bandit <Strikes again!/Ha-Ha-Ha>

ORDER HERE

RATINGS

Legality Rating: **4-CD**

Availability: **12/60 days**

Street Index: **4**

MPCP

As in regular cyberdecks, the master persona control program chip, or MPCP, as it is more commonly known, is the heart of the cranial cyberdeck (colloquially referred to as a C^2 deck, or just C^2). The MPCP controls all actions performed by the C^2 deck, including persona appearance and the regulation of the two-way simsense/cybernetic interface. Programs that are intended to be run within the C^2 system cannot have a rating higher than the level of the internal MPCP unit.

The maximum rating of an installed MPCP cannot exceed 1.5 times the subject's Intelligence Attribute (rounded up). Anything installed that is higher than the maximum rating results in a target number penalty for all actions of +4, across the board (i.e., all dice rolls).

In almost all cases C^2 decks operate exactly like regular cyberdecks. A decker may shift his MPCP Rating on the fly for purposes of lowering the C^2's Load Rating. As with the regular cyberdeck, this takes one Action to perform, and the MPCP Rating may be changed to any value less than or equal to its "real" rating. This may also entail a consequential change in the rating of the C^2's persona module. A C^2 deck may also be run in any of the five modes available to a regular cyberdeck (normal running mode, bod mode, evasion mode, masking mode, and sensor mode). See p. 35, **Virtual Reality** for more details.

Essence Cost:
(MPCP Rating/10) + .1

Construction:
MPCP Rating^3 x 200¥ + 1,250¥ (for matrixware simsense chip)

Base Time: (Rating^2) x 12
Build Time: Rating x 5
Appropriate Skills [Target]
  Design: Average of Computer and Cybernetics
    Skill Ratings (round down)
  Building: Average of Computer (B/R) and
    Cybernetics (B/R) Skills (round down)
Tools Required: Microtronics Shop, Cybernetics Shop, Optical Chip Encoder, Personal Computer (minimum MP equal to Rating^2 x 6)
Cost: (Rating^3) x 200¥

Limits:
  Max Rating = Average of designer's Computer Skill and Cybernetics Skill
  (round down)

Upgrade:
  Design: (New – Old)
  Build (New)

Note: Build Time replaces Cook Time. It incorporates Cook Time, plus the time for building the actual cybernetic systems.

>>>>>[Chummer, I really gotta get me one of these cranial cyberdecks.]<<<<<
    —Findler-Man <10:21:06/12-15-52>

>>>>>[Do it. It's worth every nuyen. Just the fact that you no longer have to lug around an external box is reason enough. No more worries about having your deck shot up, stolen, or left behind. It's a lot of freedom.]<<<<<
    —The Smiling Bandit <Strikes again!/Ha-Ha-Ha>

PERSONA MODULE

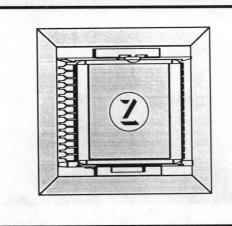

ORDER HERE

RATINGS °

Legality Rating: **4-CD**
Availability: **See below/
12 days**
Street Index: **See below**

Persona modules are unique in C² construction because they may be removed and replaced without need for additional surgery. Housed in a recessed and covered external jack/port, the module contains the persona programs essential to C² operations: bod, evasion, masking, and sensors.

Cranial cyberdeck "Body" is controlled by bod. Bod is used normally as the target number for attacking Intrusion Countermeasures.

Evasion is the attribute used when attempting to evade unauthorized programs and commands from IC. It is analogous in some ways to a node's Security Rating.

The ability to blend in with the Matrix nodes is a function of masking. Masking helps the decker defeat various tracer and identification programs.

Lastly, sensor mode gives the deck's persona the ability to detect things and events that happen within the Matrix.

A persona module's maximum rating is equal to 75 percent of the C²'s MPCP rating (rounded down). All programs contained within the module function at levels equal to the module's rating. For example, a persona module 4 operates as Bod 4, Evasion 4, Masking 4, and Sensor 4.

Level	Essence Cost	Construction Cost	Street Availability*	Street Price
1–3	.30	Level^2 x 1,000¥	Con. Cost/10,000	Con. Cost x Availability**
4–6	.30	Level^2 x 5,000¥	Con. Cost/10,000	Con. Cost x Availability**
7–9	.30	Level^2 x 10,000¥	Con. Cost/10,000	Con. Cost x Availability**
10+	.30	Level^2 x 50,000¥	Con. Cost/10,000	Con. Cost x Availability**

*Round up, minimum of 4.
**Minimum multiple 5.5.

Raw Code Size: (Rating^2 x 12 Mp)
Base Time: Size x 8 days
Build Time: Rating x 14 days
Appropriate Skills [Target]
    Computer (Rating x 1.5)
Tools Required: Personal Computer or better (minumum memory equal to size); Persona Module part
Part Cost: (Persona Module) Rating^2 x 50¥

Limits:
Max Rating equal to designer's Computer Skill

Upgrade: Desired Rating, Difference in Base Time

Through customization, each of the four separate programs (bod, evasion, masking, and sensor) may be set to distinct levels. The total levels within the module must remain equal to (or less than) four times the module's level. Within a Level 5 persona module, for example, the total levels for functions must remain equal to, or less than, 20.

The base time to complete each customization is a number of days equal to twice the modified level; the Target Number for the Computer B/R Success Test is equal to the modified level. To make a change to Bod 6, for example, requires a successful Computer B/R (6) Test and a base time of 12 days. Any Success Test that results in failure destroys the persona module.

>>>>>[With some creative tinkering, it's possible to customize persona modules to individual specifications.]<<<<<
—The Smiling Bandit <Strikes again!/Ha-Ha-Ha>

HARDENING

RATINGS

Legality Rating: **4-CD**
Availability: **See below/ 8 days**
Street Index: **See below**

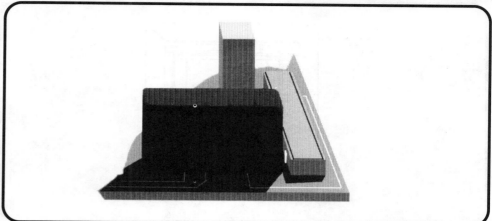

Hardening is "armor" for the C² deck. Hardening involves the application of a number of software and hardware techniques to keep damage from penetrating to the C²'s MPCP. If the persona suffers damage, the C²s Hardening Rating is applied as automatic successes in an effort to reduce the effect of the attack. Hardening is applied before the MPCP makes its Resistance Test.

The maximum rating for Hardening is equal to one-half the value of the MPCP (round down).

Essence Cost
.3

Construction Cost
MPCP rating^2 x Hardening Level^4 x 2¥

Street Availability*
Con. Cost/10,000

Street Price
Con. Cost x Availability**

*Round up, minimum 4.
**Minimum multiple of 5.5.

Base Time: MPCP x (Rating^2) x 5
Build Time: MPCP x Rating
Appropriate Skills [Target]
    Design: Average of Computer and Cybernetics
    Skills (round down) [Rating + MPCP]
       Building: Average of Computer (B/R) and
       Cybernetics (B/R) Skills (round down) [Rating +MPCP]
Tools Required: Microtronics Shop, Cybernetics Shop, Optical Chip Encoder, Personal Computer (minimum Mp equal to MPCP x Rating x 5)

Limits:
Max Rating = One-half MPCP (round down)
Upgrade:
    Design— (New – Old)
    Build— (New)

>>>>>[Hardening is like having a permanently active shield program. No combat deck should be without it.]<<<<<
   —Fastjack <14:22:15/12-15-52>

MEMORY/STORAGE

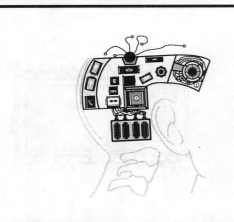

ORDER HERE

RATINGS

Legality Rating: **Legal**

Availability: **3/24 hours**

Street Index: **.8**

In most circumstances, the cranial cyberdeck uses regular headware memory as C^2 active and storage memory. Because of its custom-processing scheme, the C^2 deck can only access an amount of dedicated headware memory as active memory equal to its MPCP Rating x 50 Mp. It is not possible to use this memory for any other purpose. Additional headware memory, up to an accessible maximum equal to the MPCP Rating x 100 Mp, can be used as storage memory. Any remaining headware memory beyond this can still be used for other, more standard purposes. Active and storage headware memory operate exactly as standard active and storage memory.

Data storage is usually handled offline. It requires a datajack to use this kind of device, but the storage unit must be connected via the datajack in order to be accessed. Load Speed for offline storage is determined by the Datajack's DFR (to a maximum rating of MPCP x 10 Mp per turn).

Active and storage memory use the Legality and Availability Codes of headware memory and standard optical chips, respectively. Users need merely expend an Action to redistribute programs between active and storage memory at an equivalent Load Speed equal to the MPCP x 5 Mp per Action.

Type	Essence Cost	Price
Headware	Mp/300	Mp x 150¥

>>>>>[I once knew a guy who tried to interface one of the early brain-decks with sufficiently high-speed external memory for use as active storage. Unfortunately, it never quite worked right. The processor subroutines kept misplacing code packets as it re-mapped the memory. Fraggin' annoying. Too bad no one's ever been able to pull it off since.]<<<<
—Findler-Man <16:01:28/12-15-52>

>>>>>[That's not entirely true.]<<<<<
—Fastjack <17:56:09/12-15-52>

ORDER HERE

RATINGS

Legality Rating: **4-CD**
Availability: **See below/**
10 days
Street Index: **See below**

TRANSFER

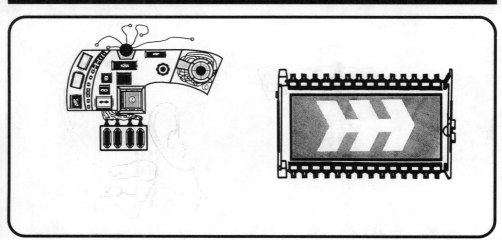

A cranial cyberdeck's Transfer Rating is synonymous with a regular deck's Input/Output speed. It is a measure of how capable the deck is at moving data around in the Net. Transfer is measured in megapulses per turn. (For example, Transfer 50 indicates that the C^2 unit may manipulate data at a rate of 50 Mp per turn.) If the connection is made through the subject's datajack (which is likely in most cases), the "real" transfer speed will be limited to a maximum rate equal to the Datajack's DFR, and may never exceed the jack's DFR. When interfacing through a Level 4 datajack, for example, "real" transfer is limited to a maximum rate of 100 Mp/turn regardless of "actual" transfer speed.

Essence Cost	Construction Cost	Street Availability	Street Cost
.1	MPCP x Transfer x 75¥	Con. Cost/10,000*	Con. Cost x Availability**

*Round up. Minimum 4.
**Minimum multiple of 5.5.

Base Time: (MPCP x Transfer)/5
Build Time: (MPCP x Transfer)/10
Appropriate Skills [Target]
    Lower of Computer or Cybernetics Skill
    [(MPCP x Transfer)/50)]
Tools Required: Microtronics Shop, Cybernetics Shop, Optical Chip Encoder, Personal Computer [minimum Mp equal to (MPCP x Transfer)/10]

Limits:
    Max Transfer = MPCP x 10
Upgrade:
    Design: (New – Old)
    Build: (New)

>>>>>[Bummer, at the high-end, effective transfer speed seems to be dictated by the datajack's data flow rate.]<<<<<
    —Findler-Man <18-21-49/12-15-52>

RESPONSE

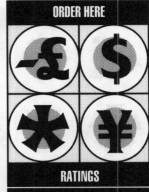

ORDER HERE

RATINGS

Legality Rating: **4-CD**
Availability: **See below/**
14 days
Street Index: **See below**

Response is the cyberdeck equivalent of wired reflexes (augmenting the decker's Reaction Attribute while running the Matrix). Response increases the reaction capability of the C^2 deck in which it is installed. Each level of Response adds +2 to Reaction and a +1D6 to the Initiative Roll when the subject is in the Matrix.

Essence Cost	Construction Cost	Street Availability*	Street Cost**
.2	MPCP^2 x Response^2 x 100¥	Con. Cost/10,000	Con. Cost x Availability

*Round up. Minimum 4.
**Minimum multiple 5.5.

Base Time: (MPCP x Response^2) x 10
Build Time: (MPCP x Response)/5
Appropriate Skills [Target]
    Design: Lower of Computer or Cybernetics Skills
      [MPCP + Response]
    Build: Lower of Computer (B/R) or
      Cybernetics (B/R) Skills (MPCP + Response)
Tools Required: Microtronics Shop, Cybernetics Shop, Optical Chip Encoder, Personal Computer [minimum Mp equal to (MPCP x Response x10]

Limits:
    Max Response = MPCP/4 (round down)
Upgrade:
    Design: New
    Build: New

>>>>>[Zoom.]<<<<<
   —Findler-Man <22:57:11/12-15-52>

ORDER HERE

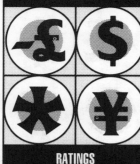

RATINGS

Legality Rating: **Legal**

Availability: **4/6 days**

Street Index: **1**

CHEMICAL ANALYZER

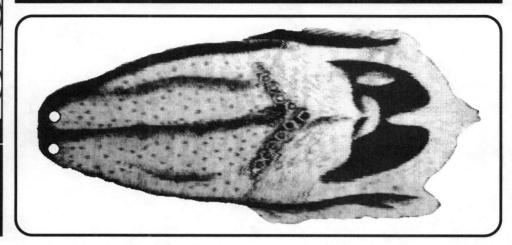

The chemical analyzer is usually implanted in the tongue or in a fingertip. This device requires a small sample of the compound to be analyzed in order to determine its chemical composition. The sample may be in any solid or liquid form (powder, liquid, aqueous solution, and so on). In most instances the amount of sample required for analysis is not enough to inflict damage or harm to the appendage or user (subject to gamemaster discretion). When used by itself, the chemical analyzer will provide only the raw chemical breakdown or composition. In conjunction with a chemical reference program (50 Mp/7,500¥), the analyzer also provides common and/or industrial compound names, and will prepare a short précis on the application and properties of the material in question. (Only one copy of this program is needed if the subject has both a chemical analyzer and a gas spectrometer). A display link or a datajack is required for output. For purposes of analysis, the analyzer functions at a Chemistry Skill Level equal to its rating + 2. For example, a Level 4 chemical analyzer performs at Chemistry Skill 6 to determine a compound's composition.

Essence Cost   **Price**
.2   2,500¥/level (maximum 6)

>>>>>[Yes, now you too can find out exactly what goes into all those Mr. Soy burgers.]<<<<<
—Winger <11:46:23/12-16-52>

>>>>>[Not to mention what's in all that junk food.]<<<<<
—Digger <13:05:54/12-16-52>

>>>>>[Airt mae, yog aer un Twinkie.]<<<<<
—Patrick <14:37:03/12-16-52>

GAS SPECTROMETER

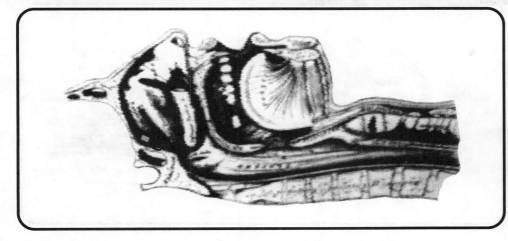

ORDER HERE

RATINGS

Legality Rating: **Legal**

Availability: **4/5 days**

Street Index: **1**

Housed in the main sinus chambers, a gas spectrometer is used to provide an analysis of the chemical composition of gases. Only a small sample is needed for analysis; usually a small sniff will suffice. Under most circumstances, the amount of gas required for analysis will not be enough to inflict damage or harm on the user (subject to gamemaster discretion). For purposes of chemical identification and analysis, the spectrometer functions at a Chemistry Skill Level equal to its rating +2. By itself, the gas spectrometer will provide only the raw chemical breakdown of a gaseous mixture. When used in conjunction with a chemical reference program (50 Mp/7,500¥), the spectrometer provides common and/or industrial compound names, and also prepares a short précis on the application and properties of the gas in question. (Only one copy of this program is required if the subject has both a gas spectrometer and a chemical analyzer.) A display link or datajack is required for output.

Essence Cost	Price
.2	2,000¥/level (maximum 6)

>>>>>[Why would I want to know the chemical composition of the air I'm breathing? Kinda useless, if you ask me.]<<<<<
— Rapid Fire <15:09:15/12-16-52>

>>>>>[Actually, you can get a lot of information from sampling the air. Personal scents, for instance, can remain in the air and provide a useful trail for a number of hours (depending on traffic through the area and the prevailing weather patterns).]<<<<<
— Feral <17:24:00/12-16-52>

OLFACTORY BOOSTER

ORDER HERE

RATINGS

Legality Rating: **Legal**

Availability: **6/6 days**

Street Index: **1**

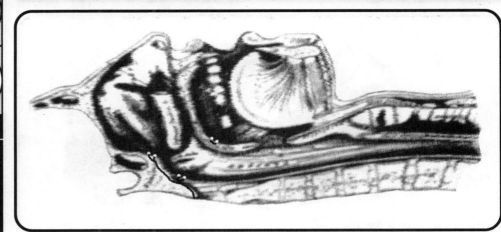

An olfactory booster is actually a combination of a number of small receptors set into the nasal passages and at the back of the mouth. Each level of olfactory booster adds 1 die to any Perception Tests to identify or detect a smell. Moreover, as taste is associated with smell, every three levels (round up) of olfactory booster will also add 1 die to Perception Tests for taste. Olfactory boosters contain high-level safety cut-offs to prevent discomfort and distraction from intense odors. In effect, the olfactory sense (and to some degree, the sense of taste as well) can be shut off.

Essence Cost	Price
.2	1,000¥/level (maximum 6)

>>>>>[This can get pretty disgusting.]<<<<<
　　—Digger <18:01:01/12-16-52>

>>>>>[Well, then, stop sticking your nose where it doesn't belong.]<<<<<
　　—The Smiling Bandit <Strikes again!/Ha-Ha-Ha>

ORIENTATION SYSTEM

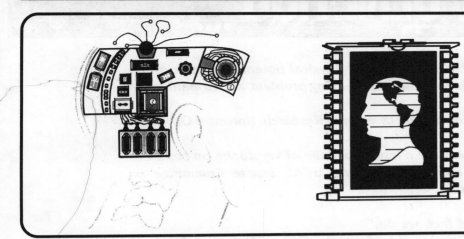

Actually a two-part system, a complete Orientation System consists of a mapping unit connected to an inertial/magnetic positioning system and a display link or a datajack for output. Data for the mapping unit is provided via a special integral chipjack that accepts only map datasofts. These are available at varying prices, depending on map completeness and complexity. A basic city street map costs 250¥, a city block map including sewage/gas/electricity/maintenance accessways, is 1,000¥; a single, intricately detailed building map costs 750¥ (subject to availability), and so on. When the appropriate softmap is interfaced, the user's exact positioning and elevation relative to sea level can be displayed. Note that street level can also be used as a point of reference when referring to elevation, as in 15 meters above street level, 5 meters below street level, and so forth. Because the softmap is a dedicated system, its size does not affect SLD or SSLD in any way.

The synergy between the orientation system and the tactical computer is evident. With both installed, the host gets more accurate tracking, and the tactical computer can provide more accurate trajectory predictions (having the complete map available on which to make its projections).

Essence Cost	Price
.50	15,000¥

EUGENICS/GENETICS

"Try not to focus on the purely physical potentials. Think of the benefits to disease control, the aging problem, and to mankind in general."
—**Dr. Kristine Martin, Director of Research, Universal Omnitech**

"I just hope you have a large stockpile of kryptonite on hand."
—**Senator Padraic von Thorn, UCAS Senate Committee on Corporate Affairs**

"As a matter of fact, we do."
—**St. John Smythe, Chief Executive Officer, Universal Omnitech**

According to *Webster's New World Dictionary*, College Edition, 2049, genetics is "the branch of biology that deals with heredity and variation in similar and related animals and plants." The same *Webster's* defines eugenics as "the science dealing with the improvement of races and breeds through the control of hereditary factors." In the year 2052 many corporations have their own definitions of these same sciences. They might say genetics is "an investment in technological superiority" and that eugenics is "a method by which one can cash in on said technological superiority."

Whatever the definitions, both genetics and eugenics involve the study of genes, and thus of life. DNA, or deoxyribonucleic acid, is commonly referred to as the blueprint for life. A self-replicating double helical structure, DNA carries the genes upon which all terrestrial life is based. A being's genes are the ultimate expression of what he or she is physically. To control's one's genes is literally to take one's future into hand.

THE STRANGER WITHIN

All living things (animals, plants, and all things in between) are made of cells. In each cell is an enclave where the materials necessary for cellular activity and reproduction reside. This enclave is called the nucleus.

Within the nucleus are masses of genetic material called chromosomes, the number varying from organism to organism. Humans and metahumans have 23 pairs of chromosomes, fruit flies have four pairs, and bacteria have but a single unpaired length. Chromosomes are collections of genes, which are the basic units of heredity. The genetic information for human/metahuman physiology spreads out over 100,000 individual genes, while the information for a virus may be contained in as few as six. An organism's genetic repertoire contains genes that specify various cellular and organismic functions. Some code for protein synthesis, biochemical conversions, or complex developmental processes (shaping and forming a developing embryo, for example), while others dictate the behavioral attributes of an organism. Genes themselves are located on double-stranded molecules of DNA,

>>>>>[Hey, doc, I know biotech is a huge and continually growing concern, but exactly how big are we talking about here?]<<<<<
—Digger <06:11:56/12-17-52>

>>>>>[I'm not at liberty to discuss exact figures, so suffice it to say that discoveries in genetic technology are constantly changing the way the world works.]<<<<<
—KAM <11:58:02/12-17-52>

>>>>>[According to my figures, Universal Omnitech spent 31.8 billion nuyen in the pursuit of genetic research alone in the last fiscal year.]<<<<<
—The Smiling Bandit <Strikes again!/Ha-Ha-Ha>

>>>>>[Not to confirm or deny any allegations, but where do you get your information, Mr. Bandit?]<<<<<
—KAM <13:33:29/12-17-52>

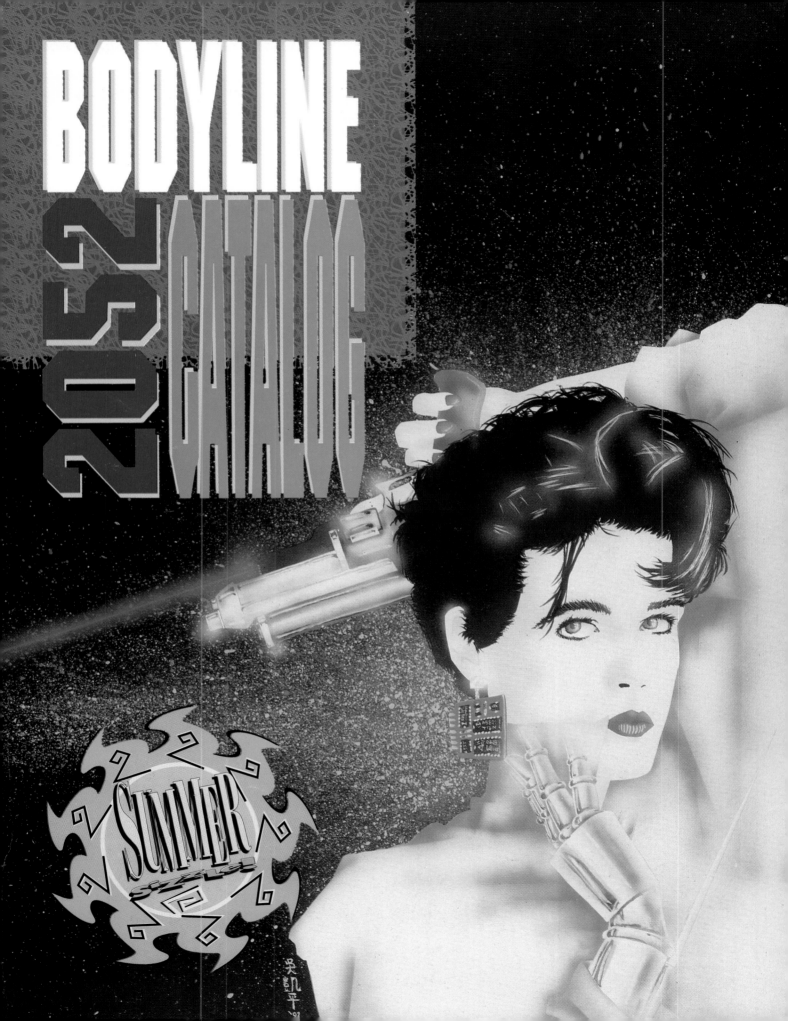

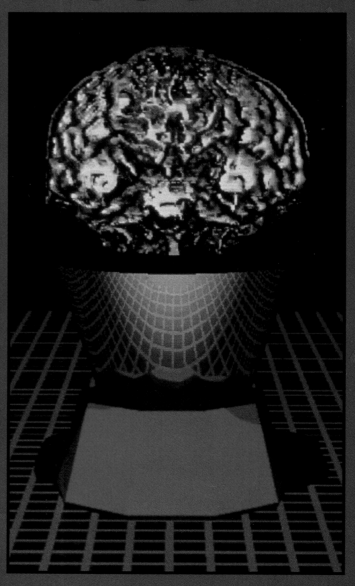

The Spinal Tap to Performance!

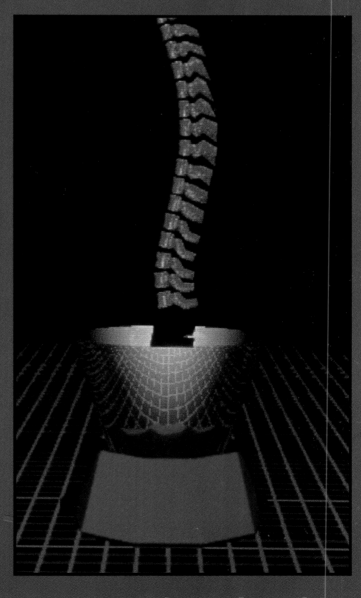

WITH PLAYBACK™, BIOTECHNICS' NEW REFLEX-RECORDING SYSTEM, THINGS YOU NEVER DREAMED YOU WERE CAPABLE OF BECOME INSTINCTIVE. ANYONE CAN PLAY A SPORT JUST LIKE A REAL PROFESSIONAL, AND WITHOUT YEARS OF TRAINING.

IF SOMEONE'S BODY CAN DO IT, SO CAN YOURS, WITH PLAYBACK™.

BioTechnics© Eyes, ears, and toes above the rest.

Does your Brain need a boost?

WITH BIOTECHNICS'
INTERNALLY APPLAUDED
ENCEPAHALON!™ SYSTEM,
THE VAST, UNTAPPED
RESOURCES OF YOUR BRAIN
ARE YOURS TO EXPLOIT.

MORE INFORMATION,
FASTER PROCESSING,
BETTER DATA STORAGE—
EVERYTING MOTHER NATURE
SKIMPED ON IS YOURS,
ON DEMAND.

BioTechnics© Building the Better You.

HAPPY JACKZ

HEY ZYMOT!!!
JOHNNIE
SPINRAD

CYBERNETIC
ENHANCEMENTS
ARE JUST THE
THING TO GET
YOU WIRED.

753 REX

NOT JUST RAD
SPINRAD!

EVERYTHING FOR YOUR C³ INCLUDING:
MPCPS
HARDENING
PERSONA MODULES
TRANSFER & RESPONSE OPTIONS
MEMORY/STORAGE UPGRADES

LTG# X312 (43-6515)

APPOINTMENTS BY
REFERRAL ONLY

which comprises the bulk of chromosomal material. The particular ordering of chemicals in a segment of DNA determines the exact content of information stored in a given gene.

DNA controls heredity by controlling the chemical and structural composition of the organism itself. This is generally achieved by controlling the sequence of amino acids that make up individual proteins. Just as DNA may be termed the blueprint for life, proteins can be viewed as the building blocks of life. Proteins, which are the primary component of cells, are omnipresent throughout the body. Hair, skin, bones, hormones, antibodies, and enzymes are all proteins. By altering the proteins present in an organism, one inevitably alters the basic structure and operation of that being.

The key to DNA's control lies in its structural composition. DNA exists as a long molecular chain of bonded nucleotides. Nucleotides are themselves comprised of three smaller bonded groups: a sugar group (deoxyribose), a phosphate group, and a nitrogen-containing compound referred to as a base. In DNA, the base can be any one of the following: adenine (A), cytosine (C), guanine (G), or thymine (T). As there are only four different nitrogenous bases, only four distinct types of nucleotides can join together to form DNA (each labeled and categorized as A, C, G, or T, according to their nitrogenous base content).

These nucleotides are further grouped into units called codons. Each codon consists of three sequential nucleotides, and, as a whole, represent the smallest unit of recognizably "meaningful" genetic information. With three nucleotides making up the codon module, and with four distinct possibilities for each nucleotide in the group, there exist a total of 64 unique combinations for codon composition. Of these 64, only 20 have a corresponding amino acid relation. The others are start/stop codes, buffers, and other control segments.

Proteins are complex chains of amino acids. By varying the length of the chain and the amino acids that constitute its composition, different proteins are created. This production of a protein from a gene is termed "expression of the gene." As the pattern of codons describes the sequence of events and amino acids involved in protein synthesis, and as the structure of each codon is in turn governed by the sequence of the individual nucleotides, changing the pattern of nucleotides that form the basis of DNA will change the types of proteins produced by a given cell. If the change is system-wide, the alterations affect the proteins generated by the organism as a whole.

Considering the enormous role played by proteins in body composition and chemistry, a change in the proteins expressed changes the entire nature and functioning of the organism with it.

GENETIC ENGINEERING

Changing the DNA nucleotide sequence is the basis of gengineering. Altering the commands for protein synthesis will create new/different proteins. By changing the proteins that constitute an organism, the organism is changed by default, creating a new strain, or even, perhaps, an entirely different species. This is the ultimate end of gengineering: the manipulation of living organisms.

One method used to control the nucleotide sequence involves the use of DNA-cleaving enzymes known as restriction endonucleases (often referred to simply as restriction enzymes). Restriction enzymes latch onto segments of the DNA chain and cut it open. This split produces a phenomenon called "sticky ends," breaks in the chain that are prone to bonding/closure. This process makes it possible to add or remove segments of code, after which the sticky ends are rebonded (thereby reunifying the DNA chain). Though the procedure was a powerful tool for genetic manipulation at the time of its discovery in 1973, its drawbacks limit current usefulness. Restriction enzymes are very precise and will cleave DNA only at very specific sites. For example, the enzyme EcoRI cuts only where it encounters a GAATTC fragment in the DNA chain, and SmaI only cleaves at CCCGGG, and so forth. Though there are 400 known restriction endonucleases, they splice DNA at only 100 different junctions. Greater access to the DNA must be achieved in order to facilitate more serious and dedicated organismic changes.

Genetic rearrangement is now performed by means of microscopic, single-celled "machines" called nanites. Nanites have themselves been genetically altered to seek out specific sites and cleave the DNA open at these spots. Other types of nanites are then used either to insert the desired segments or to remove unwanted code before the sticky ends are resealed. Because the cleaving nanites can be "programmed" to locate any sequence desired, gengineering has become quite an exact science.

Genotypic change begins at a subcellular level, starting with one cell and spreading slowly to eventually encompass the organism as a whole. The entire genetic component of an organism must be converted to the new sequence if the change is to affect the subject as a single unit. The larger and more internally complex the structure of an organism, the lengthier and more difficult it is to change on a base genetic level. Optimally, the subject of a gengineering project would be a single-celled, fast-gestating organism such as a bacteria or

>>>>>[That, doctor, would be telling.]<<<<<
—The Smiling Bandit <Strikes again!/Ha-Ha-Ha>

>>>>>[I recently saw some strange things flying over a site about 25 miles west of DeeCee. Some more of your handiwork, Doctor M?]<<<<<
—Winger <15:17:40/12-17-52>

>>>>>[There are no secrets these days, eh? You must be talking about the bloats. No, those are a Genecraft design. They're airborne cargo craft, based on a modified jellyfish platform. Relatively slow as far as airspeed is concerned, but able to carry an incredible amount of cargo from point to point. As far as I know, they're still working out some significant design problems.]<<<<<
—KAM <18:04:59/12-17-52>

virus. It is not always possible, prudent, or desirable to work exclusively with such micro-organisms, however. The great push at the moment is for more work on gengineering multi-celled (macrobiological) organisms. Most of the work on complex organisms has been performed on "lower" mammalian species, however, because results are achieved at a faster rate with smaller life forms. With lesser amounts of genetic material to change over, the accompanying reproductive cycle is faster. Even when working on these relatively "simple" complex organisms, it is easier to perform changes when dealing with the germ cells (sperm and egg cells), the most elemental cells of life. Germ-line insertion involves specifically altering the germ cells that transmit genetic information from parent to offspring. With this method, it is only necessary to change one cell's contents in order for the modifications to become organism-wide. Depending on the complexities of the desired change, however, it can still take several of the organism's generations, many years, and enormous amounts of capital investment to perfect species gengineering.

Species gengineering for "higher" complex life forms (specifically, humans and metahumans) is hideously complex and therefore a relatively long-term goal for both researchers and corporations. This is not to say, however, that there are currently no genetic engineering techniques affecting such organisms; methods for treating cellular and genetically linked diseases and similarly manifesting conditions do exist and fall under the realm of gene therapy.

Gene therapy is not so much a radical genetic redefinition as it is genetic correction. Its ability to produce drastic change is limited by the fact that internal biochemistry has already been set in organisms past the germ stage. To change the cellular functions at such a late developmental phase would either kill the being outright or make it critically ill, with little chance of recovery. Thus, alterations done by gene therapy must fall within the standard operational norms and boundaries of the species in question.

Even with such limitations, gene therapy can be a very powerful instrument. By first making an initial genetic probe, the geneticist can isolate "problem" areas in the subject's genetic map. These "faulty" segments are then altered via nanite surgery to eliminate the "detrimental" conditions. In conjunction with other treatments, gene therapy can be used to treat any genetic "defects" and cellular anomalies, including cancer, sickle cell anemia, damage caused by mutanegenic compounds, and so on.

Theoretically, even the disruption caused by VITAS (Virally Induced Toxic Allergy Syndrome) and the changes wrought through UGE (Unexplained Genetic Expression) could be tackled by dedicated gene therapy. Depending on the extent and complexity of change in the genetic condition (in relation to the "normal" species base-line model), gene therapy can be a long, arduous, and expensive process. Correction of VITAS- and UGE-related conditions, for instance, would be extremely extensive and would, therefore, be protracted and difficult by definition.

Gene therapy is usually only applied to repair damage or correct a condition that is still unmanifest. In certain circumstances, such as cancer, VITAS, or any other genetically volatile development, it can be used in conjunction with the specific neutralization processes. With gene therapy, the alterations are somatic, affecting the organism's entire genetic structure, including the reproductive tissues. Thus, any changes made through gene therapy are passed onto the subject's successive generations. Correction achieved through gene therapy is permanent, and, barring further exposure to mutanegenic compounds or conditions, not subject to reoccurrence of any nature.

>>>>>[The military's got a modified version of the bloat in development; it's based on a man-o'-war genome. Pretty nasty business.]<<<<<
　　—The Smiling Bandit <Strikes again!/Ha-Ha-Ha>

>>>>>[What about some gengineered critters with paranormal abilities?]<<<<<
　　—Findler-Man <19:52:07/12-17-52>

>>>>>[Playing around with magically active genomes is still a hit-or-miss proposition. Any success usually comes from "lifting" meta-coding straight from a parent genome. We're still very much in the dark about how genes channel astral energies.]<<<<<
　　—KAM <07:48:18/12-18-52>

THE GENOME INITIATIVE

To make changes in an organism, a blueprint of sorts must exist in order to direct the "renovation" with any precision or accuracy.

Genome is the label used to describe a genetic blueprint. It refers to the sequence of nitrogenous bases that comprise the structure of genetic material in an organism. For humans and metahumans this involves a sequence of more than three billion base pairs. The two processes involved in acquiring a complete and useful genome are called mapping and sequencing.

A physical map of the genome consists of a collated list of the DNA fragments that span the entire genome and whose positions on the chromosomes are known. This data leads to identifying which genes are associated with an organism's particular features, such as protein synthesis, disease suscepti-bility, and so forth. As for completeness and complexity, mapping is akin to a software developer drawing up a flow chart for a program; the processes and their results are known, but little else.

Sequencing gives the exact order in which each of the bases occur in the genome. This process provides much more information about how genetic information is expressed and how particular cells work. Using the computer-programming metaphor once more, sequencing would be similar to the developer writing the actual program, that is, producing the source code based on someone else's idea/plan.

Having a map and a sequence are not mutually inclusive states. For example, it is entirely possible to have a map of the genome and to know that a certain fragment of DNA codes for a specific hereditary disease, yet still not be sure of the exact sequence of nucleotides that make up the control codes. Similarly, one can have a genome completely sequenced, but not know what sections code for any given trait. In short, knowing what segments code for specific features and how those fragments are encoded are two separate functions.

Ever since James Watson and Francis Crick discovered the structure of DNA in 1962, scientists have theorized about the benefits of genetic engineering. But it was not until complete genomes of all the organisms in question were available that any serious work could be accomplished. The year 1985 saw the beginning of a period of scientific research now known as the "genome initiative." At this time, geneticists the world over began work acquiring the complete genomes of all the crea-tures found in Earth's ecosphere. Most of the work inevitably centered around the human genome.

With the introduction of the scanning tunneling micro-scope (STM) in the early 1990s, sequencing genetic information became a relatively simple matter of using an STM probe to read the three-dimensional shapes of DNA molecules into research super-computers and then translating the resulting image into a chemical chain (each nucleotide having its own unique shape). A single test-subject's DNA could be scanned and sequenced in its entirety in as little as ten to 48 hours, the time differing proportionally depending on how much genetic material was involved. Work on deciphering the blueprints for life continued apace until the upheavals in world politics and economics took its toll on the scientific community. With the breakup and collapse of several governments beginning in 2011, the ge-nome initiative soon lost most of its major funding and support: money and power were being diverted elsewhere in an effort to stabilize the chaos that threatened to engulf the world.

The research was neither forgotten nor given up, however. Several corporations bought up all the work they could find on the current state of the genome initiative, continuing the avenues of study in privately funded laboratories. Although the pace of research slowed considerably, by 2046 three different megacorporations (Aztechnology, Shiawase, and Universal Omnitech) had announced publicly that they had fully decoded the mundane segments of the human/metahuman genome.

Outside of the human species, 38 percent of the Earth's life forms have now been fully mapped and sequenced. This number consists mostly of bacteria, viruses, and other lower life forms. In addition, the DNA of another 14 percent of the planet's life forms has been completely sequenced and catalogued, though their genomes have yet to be mapped and correlated.

Just having a full genome of an organism, however, is not enough. The genome must be translated and understood before anyone can radically alter an existing organism or gengineer a new life form from scratch.

>>>>>[My investigations show that more than 97 percent of all gengineering attempts involving meta-coding result in failure or termination. The overwhelming majority of genetic work is accomplished on mundane genomes.]<<<<<
—The Smiling Bandit <Strikes again!/Ha-Ha-Ha>

>>>>>[What about those stories that are circulating about hidden installations that supposedly house all those gengineering projects gone wrong? Any truth to those stories?]<<<<<
—Feral <11:00:41/12-18-52>

>>>>>[Most of those are old runners' tales, but some are based on fact. The truth has probably been stretched in the telling.]<<<<<
—Winger <12:32:49/12-18-52>

>>>>>[Or maybe not.]<<<<<
—The Smiling Bandit <Strikes again!/Ha-Ha-Ha>

THE METAGENE

Having a complete human/metahuman genome gives insight into solving the questions surrounding the actual physiological effects of UGE and the reasons why certain individuals can tap magical/astral energies directly. Full understanding of the processes involves comprehension of current magical theory and the structure of DNA, as well as a working knowledge of chiral chemistry (the science of chemical geometry).

In nature, shape is as important as actual chemical composition—sometimes even more important. Most artificial sweeteners and sugar substitutes are, for example, not derived from sugars at all. They are usually designer proteins that mimic sugar's three-dimensional shape. To the taste receptors in the tongue, these proteins are sweet because they "look" sweet. The factors that determine a compound's physical shape include the constituent atoms and their electronegativity, bond type, bond strength and angle, and so on. The longer and more complex a molecule is, the more factors are involved in arriving at the molecule's final form. DNA, a very complex molecule with billions of constituent parts, can therefore have several billion unique shapes.

DNA's three-dimensional form is mostly controlled by the exact sequence of nucleotides that make up the whole chain. As each person has a unique genome, every individual has a unique genetic shape. However, just as every member of *homo sapiens* has common corresponding code sequences, every genome has similar "public domain" sections that take on the same physical shapes. Most of DNA's component nucleotides were once thought of as nonsense code; only a relatively small percentage of DNA corresponded to control codes or expressive code. It is now understood that these "nonsense" nucleotides are what control the ultimate shape of the complex molecule.

Magic is essentially the grounding of astral energy into the physical plane. Its specific effects and the actual channeling of the energy are accomplished with the aid of astral constructs, or spell engines. The mage determines which effect manifests through

>>>>>[There's been some discussion in the magical community that shaman's don't necessarily need to possess the magus factor. After all, shamans get most of their power from their spirit totems.]<<<<<
—MLC III <15:01:28/12-18-52>

>>>>>[Oh, very nice. That should stir the pot. Oh, and please remember all: these are a scientist's views on the states of being. No one, not even I (no comments please), am ever completely right.]<<<<<
—Minstrel H. <16:09:12/12-18-52>

>>>>>[I'm not really prepared to comment on MLC's statement. Heck, I'm not even sure that the darned thing exists at all. We've never been able to consistently or reliably quantify any real differences between individuals who can manipulate astral energies and those who cannot.]<<<<<
—KAM <18:25:43/12-18-52>

subtle alterations in the formula and construction of the specific astral engine (some segments manifest fire, others code for mind, another funnels the energy, and so on). These engines have a shape and form that are only perceptible in their totality in the dimension of magic, or astral space. A spell engine, like all other multi-dimensional objects, can be represented in a "lower" dimension by its shadow. For example, a cube is a three-dimensional shadow of a four-dimensional tessarect, just as a square is a two-dimensional shadow of a three-dimensional cube. In the case of metahumanity, the genetic configurations precisely match three-dimensional shadows of specific astral constructs.

Certain shapes within the DNA molecule code for certain corresponding metaeffects (also referred to as metatraits). For example, it is now known that a repeated GTTAATGGGATATAAGAATTGAGA fragment combined with a sulphur bond, resulting in a back-folding of the chain at 17 percent, triggers a magically active genome and the formation of scaly deposits on the dermis. Elves are *homo sapiens* whose genomes contain the correct sequence of astral shadows to bestow the *nobilis* traits. Trolls are *homo sapiens* who carry the sequence of astral shadows that code for the *ingentis* traits, and so on. These three-dimensional structures within the genome only activate in the presence of magic. That is, astral energy must be funnelled through the gene to cause this effect.

The shape fragment that codes for the direction/grounding of astral energy is called the metatrigger. Thus, a subject may have any number of astral shadows within his genome, but without an active metatrigger, he will remain completely mundane. Alternately, an individual may have a metatrigger in his structure but not the astral shadows. Such individuals develop a sensitivity to magical phenomena, but remain otherwise mundane. Although it is known that shape sequences are responsible for the various metatraits, it is not generally known at this time what patterns and what sequences of patterns correspond to specific effects. (As of 2052, only seven metatraits have been isolated and deciphered.)

Being encoded within the genome, metatraits can be classified as genetic, and thus hereditary. In the reproduction cycle, however, crossover and natural mutation may displace key spatial segments that code for specific metatraits, making the continuation of metatraits more complex than simple heredity. Therefore, metahumans do not necessarily breed true. When displacement occurs, the offspring will not necessarily be the same phenotype as its parents. Elven parents may, for example, give birth to a troll child, mundanes may give birth to a dwarf, a normal human may be the offspring of an ork line, and

so on. However, the metatraits exist in such a way that they offer no possibility for the existence of sub-races, i.e., no half-elves, half-trolls, and so forth. The child of such a union should, theoretically, be only one of the following: father's race, mother's race, other existing race, mundane, or mundane/sensitive. It is also interesting to note that while reproduction does not always breed true, certain genetic results (although theoretically possible) have *never* been documented. There has never been a properly documented case of a troll being born to elven parents, for example. The only documented relationships are as follows: father's race or mother's race, or, in the case of the *ingentis* and *robustus* expressions, the chance of a simple *sapien-sapien* that later expresses to *ingentis* or *robustus* (as appropriate for parent type) at puberty. Additionally, there continues to be a rare, very small percentage of the *sapien-sapien* population that expresses into *ingentis* or *robustus* forms at puberty, regardless of apparent heredity. Clearly, then, more is at work here than simple genetics.

As a person's genes reside along with the individual in physical three-space, the metatrigger cannot access any of the energies of astral space, but must rather draw its energy from ambient background magic. Thus, metatraits actively manifest only when the vibratory cycles of the physical plane and the astral plane achieve a harmonic point and energy flows freely between the two. At all other times, the mechanisms may be present, but there is no energy to fuel the shadow metaengines. In this sense, the metatrigger is a pleiotropic fragment, its state affecting the entire gamut of metatraits within the individual. Although the metatrigger is often referred to as the metagene, the nomenclature is incorrect. It is not a gene, but rather a spatial configuration, and its presence is not always indicative of metahuman traits.

In a magic-positive environment, an organism whose genome has both astral shadows and a functional metatrigger will develop the physical manifestations of its metatraits as soon as it can draw upon enough ambient energy to exceed the body's repression factor (for most individuals this occurs in the fetal development stage). For reasons not yet explained, the systems of certain individuals have proteins with the ability to slow down, and, in rare cases, inhibit the accumulation of the energy necessary to trigger UGE/Awakening. Depending on the individual and the specific repressor proteins present, UGE/Awakening may occur unexpectedly at any point during his/her lifetime, though usually at puberty. Once the collected energy level reaches the repression point and the metatrigger is activated, the resulting physical manifestations will remain until death.

>>>>>[Good thing, too. Can you imagine a corporate security force whose members can all cast spells?! We'd all be out of a job.]<<<<<
—The Neon Samurai <20:29:50/12-18-52>

>>>>>[This doesn't mean they've forgotten about mages. In fact, there's a specifically gengineered strain of ivy and lichen that's been developed to completely envelop an entire building and protect its occupants from astral reconnaissance attempts.]<<<<<
—The Smiling Bandit <Strikes again!/Ha-Ha-Ha>

>>>>>[I've heard someone's got a magically overactive strain of harmless bacteria that they pump though the ventilation systems of their most secure sights. Can you imagine what that must look like in astral space?]<<<<<
—Ludwig the Mad <21:45:31 12-18-52>

THE MAGUS FACTOR

While the metahuman state is dependent on the presence of overt conditions in the human genome, the magus factor, the ability to wield magicks, is a much more subtle trait. The magus factor has only a tenuous link to hereditary genetics (in as much as any mental predilection is hereditary). Studies show very little quantified physical, chemical, or biological difference between a subject who can consciously manipulate astral energies and an individual who cannot. What the magus factor grants is the ability to perceive and interact in an environment/medium other than conventional three-space. Just as certain gifted mathematicians and physical theorists can visualize and work in complex four-space, a person bearing the magus factor can perceive and interact in astral space. As with any other mental trait, the way the gifted individual views his gift and how he trains himself to best use his talent have a direct correlation on how useful the ability becomes. Individuals who can perceive the astral but who are otherwise weak-minded inevitably go insane. Others may achieve contact and then take on the role as vessels for the astral. Still others have strong enough wills that they can directly impose their own desires on the fabric of astral reality.

Pinpointing the actual genetic elements involved in bestowing the magus factor is a difficult proposition. Because of the nebulous genetic nature of the magus factor, most geneticists agree only that it exists at all. Current popular theory suggests that the magus factor is a genetic mélange, a combination of encoded mental traits (spread across the entire genome) operating in mysterious gestalt. Although geneticists have decoded and deciphered the physiological elements of man, many facets of the human mental condition (the ephemeral concepts) continue to elude identification and classification. Through gengineering, it is possible to design a human with long, delicate, and dextrous hands, perfect hearing, and excellent cerebral ability. That creation can then be taught to play a piano or any other instrument, but in almost every case the music produced will pale in comparison to that produced by a true maestro, an individual with an inborn genius for music. As with all other ephemeral characteristics found in humans, the magus factor continues to be the subject of intense research and curiosity. Every government and megacorporation in the world covets the technology that would confer the ability to isolate and control the genetic keys for magery.

APPLIED GENETICS

The application of genetic and eugenic technology for gengineering, and gene therapy of higher life-form species is by far the most glamorous and well-known, but hardly the most common, use of genetic technology. Eugenics has been put to work for more than a century in various efforts to improve the human condition. Since the early 1980s, eugenic principles and genetic technology have been directly applied to increase the quantity and quality of food production the world over. (Records from as early as the 1930s indicate that North American corn yields were increased through genetic manipulation resulting from selective breeding.) To date, more direct genetic engineering has permitted the alteration of livestock to use feed more efficiently and to mature at a faster rate; produce has been rendered immune to various diseases and pests; crops have been designed to mass more at harvest time; and gengineered bacteria, algae, and protein derivatives have sustained those who could no longer enjoy the luxury or expense of "real" food.

Modern medicine owes much of its effectiveness to developments in the field of genetics. Medicines previously expensive and hard to refine are now produced in quantity by gengineered microorganisms. The replacement organ and body-part industry exists because of "fallout" technology from genetic engineering research. Practically all bioware was developed through gengineering of one sort or another. Genetics is also responsible for the viability of cybernetics. Without the development of nanites, the integration of man and machine would have been a long time coming.

The influence of genetic technology is pervasive, touching many aspects of society in 2052. In more ways than is readily apparent, DNA has truly become the blueprint for life.

MONOCLONAL ANTIBODIES

One of the more important advances in biotechnology was the introduction of monoclonal antibodies. Antibodies are strands/clumps of protein that can identify molecules or microbes and bind to them. They are not all anti-pathogenic (disease-fighting) in nature, but that is the role most associated with antibodies. By binding to invading molecules and microbes, immune system antibodies render the foreign particles inert and mark them for destruction by the machinery of the human/metahuman immune system.

Antibodies are normally produced by white blood cells known as lymphocytes. Monoclonal antibodies are produced

>>>>>[Maybe they can't make super-mages yet, but what about super-mundanes (dwarfs, elves, humans, orks, trolls)?]<<<<<
—Feral <22:57:19/12-18-52>

>>>>>[Most of the macrobiological gengineering work done these days concerns agricultural and utility organisms. Unquestionably, many megacorporations are interested in the potentials of human gengineering, but we've just barely scratched the tip of the iceberg.]<<<<<
—KAM <07:55:09/12-19-52>

>>>>>[You mean to tell us no one's had any success with human gengineering?]<<<<<
—Winger <10:01:45/12-19-52>

>>>>>[Hey, come on. Stop giving the doc a hard time. If she wants to continue working for UO, she's going to have to keep spouting the party line.

from cells called hybridomas, which are cells created from the genetic fusion of two types of cells: tailored lymphocytes and mutated (cancerous) myeloma. Hybridomas can survive in growth mediums lacking critical nutrients (a trait inherent in their lymphocyte parents), and are effectively immortal (much like their cancer cell forefathers). Each specific strain of hybridoma will produce the particular antibody that was designed into the original tailored lymphocyte. Such antibodies are called monoclonal because they are the progeny of a single cell.

Monoclonal antibodies are highly specific, recognizing and able to react with only one type of molecule/microbe—the one for which they were designed. Because of their controllable and specific nature, monoclonal antibodies are suited to many diverse purposes: as anti-cancer agents and anticoagulants; for typing blood and identifying/treating/causing pathogenic reactions; as chemical purifiers, biological agents, for pregnancy tests, and so on. The uses of monoclonal antibodies are limited only by the imagination, and morality, of the gengineer or protein designer.

GENGINEERED BIOLOGICALS

Tailored biologicals can range in form from lowly viruses to large mammals, and are equally diverse in function. All of these "manmade" organisms have their roots in existing terrestrial species. To date, no one has been successful in producing viable life forms from genetic "scratch."

Gengineering is a formidable task. Extensive systemic changes must be introduced slowly into the existing "parent" genome to allow the new design to adapt to its new form. For that reason, radical departures from the base-line genetic model of the parental unit involve many years and several of the intended strain's filial generations to come to fruition.

Bacteria and viruses are optimal subjects for gengineering. Their extremely fast reproductive rates and growth cycles allow for numerous generational steps to occur in the course of a relatively short period. Additionally, the small amount of genetic material found within bacteria and viruses makes alteration of their genomes far simpler than manipulating higher-level organisms; there are simply fewer factors to consider and code for in single-celled life forms.

Besides, everyone practices eugenics in their own fashion. I mean, you ultimately choose to settle down with someone because you think that together you can produce and raise a beautiful family. By making that conscious decision, you're practicing human gengineering by means of selective breeding. We've been doing this for millennia. Why complain now just because someone wants to speed the process along?]<<<<<
        —The Smiling Bandit <Strikes again!/Ha-Ha-Ha>

>>>>>[Sorry doc, I just get a little overenthusiastic at times.]<<<<<
        —Winger <13:49:00/12-19-52>

>>>>>[No harm done. By the way, Mr. Bandit, you seem quite knowledgeable on a number of topics, including the current state of genetic research.]<<<<<
        —KAM <18:10:23/12-19-52>

Most variant designs never get off the computer console; few get past the first generation before succumbing to fatal design flaws. Of the remaining viable creations, more than 90 percent are based on viral and bacterial platforms, the "work-horses" of the genetic industry. The remaining share of the marketable gengineered biologicals include all the other forms of life: birds, fish, plants, reptiles, small and agricultural mammals, and so on.

OMEGA SEQUENCE #358 G

Because of the incredible complexity involved in gengineering macrobiological species, several strains are "boosted" in their development by using chimeric designs as "seed stock." A genetic chimera is an organism with genetic material from at least two genetically distinct "parents" (e.g., a cat and a chicken). The new creature reproduces itself, and carries out the genetic instructions encoded into all its inserted genes. If the design is successful, chimeric genomes reduce development time by up to 50 percent over similar genetic designs built up from only one genetic donor.

Since the unilateral ban on the continued research into biological warfare agents was set into motion in 2041, micro-biological designs have focused mainly on the industrial applications of biotechnology (drug factories, protein substitutes, refuse recyclers, and so forth). With higher-level life forms, the bulk of gengineering work involves agricultural gengineering, that is, producing better and more efficient livestock and produce. Also high on the list, in terms of both number produced and revenue from sales, are animals in the pet/curiosity and functional/utility categories. Currently, human gengineering is only in its vestigial stages.

>>>>>[We interrupt your regularly scheduled reading to bring you the following special report...

Human gengineering has gone far past the "vestigial stages" of development. There's too much potential—and too much nuyen—involved for the big corps not to have invested seriously in this line of endeavor, chummers. You can bet your trigger fingers, though, that the big boys ain't gonna tell you drek about what's really happening, how much they really know, and just how fraggin' far along they actually are. Rest assured, though, that some of us ARE watching, and will keep you posted on the latest developments in these most interesting ventures. But, do speak up if y'all run into a vat-job before the Bandit hears about it.

We now return you to your reading—already in progress.]<<<<<
—The Smiling Bandit <Strikes again!/Ha-Ha-Ha>

As time progresses and the levels of technology and understanding improve, so will the number, variety, and applications of gengineered biologicals. Species gengineering is the final word in harnessing the vast potentials of modern eugenic technology.

>>>>>[I read a lot. Comes with the territory. I've read all your papers, too. I must say that I found the Project Infinity proposal very interesting.
Oh, and doc, let me be the first to tell you that you don't look nearly old enough to have a daughter that age.]<<<<<
—The Smiling Bandit <Strikes again!/Ha-Ha-Ha>

>>>>>[Project Infinity?! Mr. Bandit, here's my home address, I think there are a few things we have to discuss, and that it's best done face to face.]<<<<<
—KAM <20:04:32/12-19-52>

>>>>>[Oh, please. That was convenient, wasn't it?]<<<<<
—Fastjack <23:11:07/12-19-52>

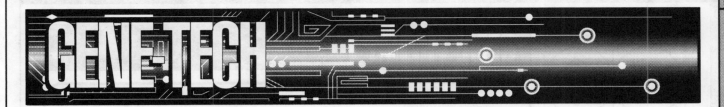

"Tell me, Doctor. Why did you decide to go into gengineering research?"
    —Alyn Vage, Reporter, Network 5 News

"To fulfill a dream mostly."
    —Dr. Terrance Clark, Gengineer, Genecraft Biodesigns

"Okay, I'll bite. What dream? A dream for a better, cleaner world? Peace on Earth? Food and care for the needy?"
    —Alyn Vage, Reporter, Network 5 News

"Nope. Redhead, five-ten with green eyes, athletic build, and legs up to here."
    —Dr. Terrance Clark, Gengineer, Genecraft Biodesigns

Marketable gene-tech products usually come in three varieties: treatments, microbiologicals, and macrobiologicals. Microbiologicals are by far the most common and least expensive type of gene-tech available.

The nature of gene-tech, however, is such that gamemasters will probably benefit more from the introduction of this technology than will players. Whether for reasons of Legality/Availability or for monetary reasons, most items are beyond the reach of the average player character. Gene-tech is more or less a tool for the gamemaster to manipulate the game, whether to make it more enjoyable, dangerous, or mysterious.

Take note that whenever a physical or mental attribute (such as Body, Intelligence, and so on) is mentioned in this section, it always refers to the subject's "natural" rating (i.e., including bioware but excluding cyberware modifiers). Anything that refers to an attribute being reduced to 0 also implies using the subject's "natural" rating. In general, when making Body Resistance Tests against pathogens and toxins, do not factor in Body derived from cyberware. Cyberware enhancements do little against biological and chemical agents.

This section contains only a small, representative listing of the available applications of gengineering technology.

>>>>>[I've seen a list of some of the stuff that's no longer available. Makes me glad to know it's under lock and key.]<<<<<
    —Digger <06:00:38/12-20-52>

>>>>>[Yeah, but who's holding the key?]<<<<<
    —Findler-Man <08:13:54/12-20-52>

ORDER HERE

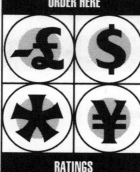

RATINGS

· Legality Rating: **Legal**

· Availability: **6/30 days**

· Street Index: **2.5**

GENE THERAPY

A catchall category that includes numerous specific procedures, gene therapy is primarily performed to correct genetic defects and problems; it can also be applied to repair body-wide cellular damage resulting from disease or toxin reaction. Depending on the case, therapy may take a single day or up to several months to complete. During the therapy process, the patient is placed in a coma-like trance while the body is immersed in a nutrient solution that contains tailored nanites. These nanites do the actual work of genetic manipulation, and differ from procedure to procedure. While in this bath, the subject cannot interact with the physical world in any way. In non-neural therapy situations, however, a subject may communicate and interact with the external world by means of a datajack (if he or she has one).

Time factors and the costs involved in gene therapy vary, depending on the desired end (correction of recessive genetic diseases, reconstructive healing, and so on). While some procedures are short and relatively inexpensive, others may be involved and costly. Regardless of how cosmetic or trivial a treatment, however, no procedure takes less than one week to complete or costs less than 50,000¥ to perform (due to absolutes in preparation and material costs).

Below is a list of sample treatments. It is suggested that individual gamemasters design and implement treatments at their own discretion.

Procedure	Time	Price
Cleansing	1 month	50,000¥
Genetic Correction	6 months	60,000¥
Reconstructive Healing	4 months	100,000¥
Other	Variable	50,000¥+

>>>>>[There's some controversy over the issue of whether or not repeated gene therapy can cause irreparable damage to the DNA code.]<<<<<
—The Smiling Bandit <Strikes again!/Ha-Ha-Ha>

>>>>>[The questions that have been raised are as yet unresolved. We don't have enough data on the repeat treatments to generate a truly fact-based conclusion.]<<<<<
—KAM <11:48:02/12-20-52>

IMMUNIZATION

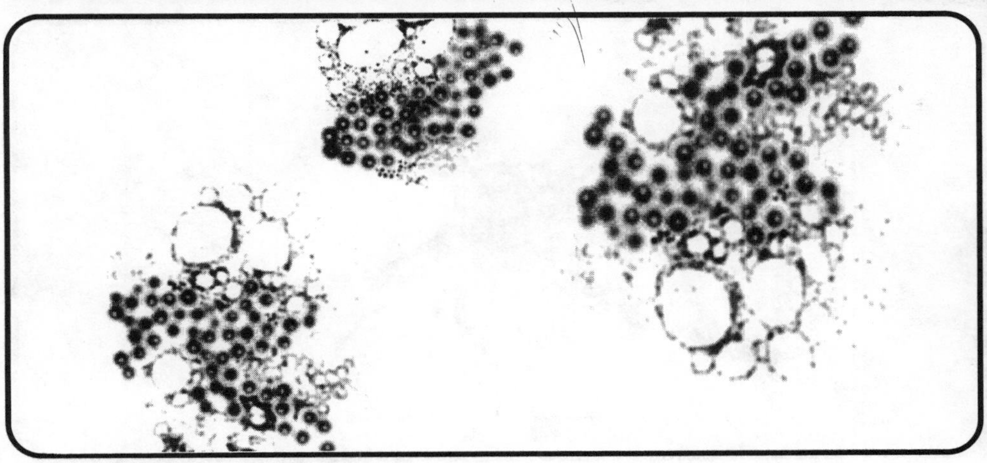

ORDER HERE

£ $

*   ¥

RATINGS

Legality Rating: **Legal**

Availability: **6/20 days**

Street Index: **2**

Immunization therapy extends a permanent immunity to a single disease or compound. This differs from standard monoclonal antibody treatment in that this procedure uses the actual hybridomas (the source of specific monoclonal antibodies) rather than just the antibodies they produce.

Immunization is a relatively simple and painless process of injecting specially tailored hybridomas into an individual's bloodstream. After a one-month incubation period, that person is immune to the effects of the particular disease or compound for which he was treated. This immunity extends only to a standard (casual) exposure to the pathogen or chemical in question, however. Highly concentrated doses (double or higher standard-strength, amount, or concentration) and mutated strains may overwhelm the targeted system to a point where infection or damage may occur. The required multiple of standard exposure level is left to the gamemaster's discretion.

A full-spectrum immunization program is also available for those who can afford it; this renders the subject immune to the effects of almost all standard-level pathogens and known toxic compounds. There has been little success in immunizing metahumans against their specific racial allergies.

Type	Price
Single	40,000¥/treatment
Full-spectrum	300,000¥

>>>>>[This is decidedly interesting...For 40,000¥, you never need suffer from the common cold again. Definitely worth thinking about.]<<<<<
    —Feral <13:24:35/12-20-52>

>>>>>[Only if the common cold were from bacterial origins. The effects of the cold are brought on by viral outbreaks. The immunization process doesn't protect against viral infection.]<<<<<
    —KAM <13:46:23/12-20-52>

LEÓNIZATION

ORDER HERE

RATINGS

Legality Rating: **Legal**
Availability: **6/30 days**
Street Index: **2.5**

Named after Ponce de León, the legendary seeker of the Fountain of Youth, Leónization treatment repairs the cellular damage that accompanies the natural aging process. This gene therapy program involves making an initial genetic probe of the subject and then preparing a nanite "bath" matched to the subject's genome. Once immersed in the nutrient solution, the body is placed in a trance-like state while the nanites go about their job of rejuvenating aged cells. This process usually takes four months to complete and is relatively fast as far as system-wide gene therapy is concerned. This is because the task at hand is simply maintenance and not any real change. Any potential (latent), genetically linked disease or condition that shows up in the initial probe of the subject may be corrected at the same time at no additional cost. During therapy, the subject cannot physically interact with others in any way. However, if he is equipped with a datajack, the subject can interact and go about his business by electronic proxy.

Leónization does not grant immortality. It is possible to successfully carry out this process only a limited number of times before the overwriting process triggers spontaneous and uncontrollable changes in the genetic code. The exact cause of this phenomenon is not yet known. The exact number of times depends on the individual; use the average of the character's Body and Willpower Ratings (rounding up) to calculate the number of times the therapy may be safely attempted. When properly administered, the treatment strips away the effects of physiological aging. For all intents and purposes, the subject's body will appear many years younger and will feel and behave as if it were in the prime of health and youth (approximately age 21). Leónization may be initiated at any time (prior to death), as there is no change in the therapy's effectiveness because of the subject's initial age. The refreshing accomplished through the process is a macroscopic physical change. No gross genomic change occurs, nor is either Body Index or Essence affected in any way.

Characters who have been treated with the Leónization process must submit to semi-annual maintenance sessions for four years following the completion of rejuvenation therapy. These maintenance sessions are mostly for fine-tuning and touch-up work, giving attending physicians and geneticists a chance to ensure that the patient has taken fully to the process. If the number of rejuvenation attempts exceeds the subject's maximum safe number of applications, the individual's cells will spontaneously degenerate. Death (after excruciating pain) comes in six hours.

Essence Cost   **Price**
.10/session   2,000,000¥/session + 100,000¥/maintenance session

>>>>>[Wiz. I can stay young and healthy for a good long time. All I need now is a way to come up with the 2.8 million nuyen for the treatment, and I'll be set for the next 80 years or so.]<<<<<
    —The Neon Samurai <15:14:21/12-20-52>

>>>>>[I just happen to know a few companies that would be glad to make a few donations to a worthy cause. Meet me at the Inferno tonight.]<<<<<
    —Winger <17:05:39/12-20-52>

ANTIBAC

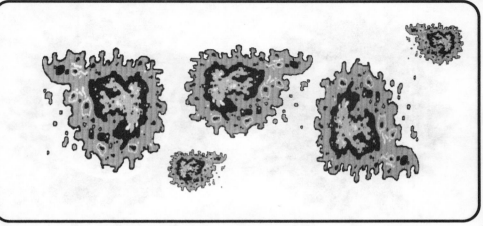

ORDER HERE

£ $

*   ¥

RATINGS

Legality Rating: **Legal**

Availability: **4/48 hours**

Street Index: **1**

Until the year 2041 the standard treatment for bacterial infections and disease were antibiotics such as amoxil, penicillin, and so forth. Though antibiotics kill the bacteria, they do not remove the endotoxins already released into the bloodstream by the bacteria. Indeed, killing the bacteria may lead to the release of even more endotoxins as the dead bacteria break apart and release the toxins contained within. A type of monoclonal antibody treatment called anti-bacteriological agent VII (or simply antibac) is now used in place of antibiotics.

Antibac protects the body from bacteremia (the presence of bacteria in the bloodstream) and endotoxic shock (the poisoning of the bloodstream by chemicals secreted by pathogenic bacteria). In the case of whole bacteria, the antibodies bind to them and mark them for destruction by the white blood cells. Antibac also binds to the secreted toxins, rendering them inert; the body then filters and expels the bonded bodies with other bodily waste.

Use of antibac will stop the progress of bacteriological disease and infection, but will not repair any damage already inflicted upon the subject's body. For resisting damage, antibac temporarily reduces the pathogen's Strength Rating by its level. For example, Level 2 antibac used against a 5M2 bacteria would reduce the damage code to 3M2. The day after antibac has been administered, the subject is allowed another Body Resistance Test against the weakened microbe. The attacking organism's Strength Rating returns to normal if the Resistance Test fails to destroy the agent.

Antibac may be administered at any time. If introduced before exposure to bacteriological agents, add half its level (round up) to the subject's Body for the appropriate Resistance Tests (i.e., versus pathogens) instead of reducing the attack's strength. Thus, Level 4 antibac will add +2 to any character's Body Attribute when resisting bacterial agents if administered before actual exposure. Antibac will remain effective in the bloodstream for only one hour after administration, and each dose is only effective for a single treatment or exposure. If an initial treatment fails, however, further attempts with antibac may still be made.

Success or failure of the antibac treatment cannot be determined immediately after administration. A period of 24 hours and a successful Biotech Success Test against a Target Number based on the bacteriological agent's strength are necessary for confirmation of antibac action (whether positive or negative). (A 6S2 microbe, for example, indicates a Target Number of 6, a 5M2 code indicates a Target Number of 5, and so on.)

Level	Price
1–3	500¥ x Level
4–6	1,000¥ x Level
7–9	1,500¥ x Level
10+	2,500¥ x Level

>>>>>[If you think you might encounter some bacterial hazards on your next run, chummers, I seriously suggest you invest in some adequately rated antibac.]<<<<<
—Reflex <19:11:20/12-20-52>

>>>>>[You can also use some of the lower-rated stuff to treat the bites and scratches from some of those nasty critters wandering around out there.]<<<<<
—Nightfire <20:38:04/12-20-52>

ORDER HERE

RATINGS

Legality Rating: **Legal**

Availability: **4/32 hours**

Street Index: **2**

BINDER

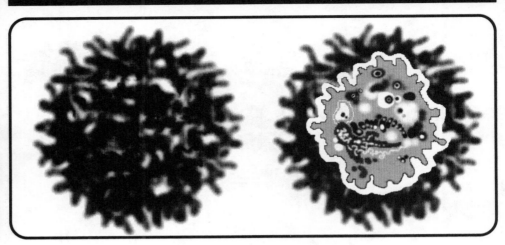

Monoclonal antibodies known as toxin binders are used to combat the effects of potentially dangerous chemicals in the bloodstream. Binder seeks out toxic compounds and attaches itself to the chemicals, rendering them inert. Binder is not usually effective against bacteriological endotoxins; antibac must be applied in such cases. Once the bonding has occurred, the body's natural defense system can either break down the "neutralized" compounds or else safely expel them through normal waste procedures.

Like all monoclonal antibody treatments, binder will halt the progress, but not help heal the damage done to the target. Unlike antibac, however, binder is toxin-specific, and must be prepared separately for each compound. Binder temporarily reduces the toxin's Strength Rating by its level in Resistance Tests. For example, Level 3 binder used against a 5D2 toxin would reduce the damage code to 2D2. Binder is fast-acting and, once administered, allows the subject an immediate Body Resistance Test against the weakened toxin. If the Resistance Test fails to neutralize the toxin, the toxin's Strength Rating returns to its normal level.

Binder may be administered at any time. If used prior to exposure, add half of binder's rating (round up) to the character's Body Attribute to determine toxin resistance against the specified compound, instead of reducing the attack's strength. (Binder administered in this fashion remains effective for only one hour.) Each dose of binder is effective for only a single treatment or exposure. If an initial treatment of binder fails, however, additional attempts may be made.

Level	Price
1–3	300¥ x Level
4–6	600¥ x Level
7–9	900¥ x Level
10+	1,500¥ x Level

>>>>>[Very effective, but much too specific to carry around with you at all times—unless, of course, you know that someone's gunning for you and is using a specific toxin.]<<<<<
    —The Neon Samurai <09:17:00/12-21-52>

>>>>>[Ah, but most people aren't even aware I'm after them—until it's far too late.]<<<<<
    —Nex <11:21:39/12-21-52>

ZETA-INTERFERON

ORDER HERE

RATINGS

Legality Rating: **Legal**

Availability: **4/32 hours**

Street Index: **2**

In cases of viral outbreaks, mammalian cells will normally produce interferons, the name given to three types of proteins (each with numerous variants). The three naturally occurring forms of interferon (alpha, beta, and gamma) are synthesized by lymphocytes and fibroblasts (with a-interferon being the most commonly encountered and produced). Interferons stimulate virally infected cells to synthesize other proteins that inhibit viral replication, slowing down and sometimes stopping the spread of infection. Interferons also make the infected cells produce "flag" proteins, which increase the chance that the body's immune system will recognize and eliminate the affected cell.

Zeta-interferon is a gengineered derivative of naturally occurring interferons. Highly specific in nature, each z-interferon is tailored to combat a single virus type or strain. Z-interferon completely halts viral replication, and the infected cells are quickly destroyed.

Similar in operation to antibac, the use of z-interferon will halt the progress and destroy the cause of viral infection, but will not help heal the damage already done to the subject's body. The z-interferon level temporarily reduces the Strength Rating of invading viruses. (After the introduction of Level 4 z-interferon, for example, a 6L2 virus reduces its code to 2L2.) Twenty-four hours after administration, the subject is allowed to make another Body Resistance Test against the weakened virus. If the Resistance Test fails to destroy the virus, however, the agent's damage code returns to its normal rating.

Zeta-interferon may be administered at any time. If used before exposure to a viral agent, add half its level to the subject's Body Rating for Resistance Tests instead of reducing the virus's Strength Rating (effectiveness in the bloodstream is only maintained for one hour). A single dose of z-interferon is effective for one treatment of exposure. If an initial treatment of z-interferon is unsuccessful, additional doses may be administered for further attempts.

Effectiveness of a z-interferon application cannot be determined immediately. A Biotech Skill Test against a Target Number equal to the viral agent's actual strength may be attempted after a period of 24 hours from the time of z-interferon administration. (In the above example of the 6L2 virus, the Target Number is 6, taken from the actual code of 6L2, not the reduced code of 2L2.) If successful, this test informs the attending physician (or user of the Biotech Skill) of either success or failure.

No form of zeta-interferon has yet been perfected that protects against the Human-Metahuman Vampiric Virus (HMVV) or the most recent form of VITAS (Virally Induced Toxic Allergy Syndrome.)

Level	Price
1–3	400¥ x Level
4–6	800¥ x Level
7–9	1,200¥ x Level
10+	2,000¥ x Level

>>>>>[Like binder, zeta-interferon is very effective, but also very specific; not something you'd want to go out and buy half a dozen of to keep on hand...just in case.]<<<<<
—The Neon Samurai <12:31:07/12-21-52>

>>>>>[Not unless you're more than a little paranoid and have more money than you know what to do with.]<<<<<
—The Smiling Bandit <Strikes again!/Ha-Ha-Ha>

ORDER HERE

RATINGS

Legality Rating: 1-M3

Availability: 14/30 days

Street Index: 5

DOOM

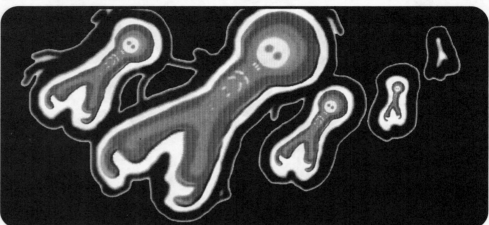

Doom is an insidious example of how monoclonal antibody technology can be dangerously abused. Gengineered doom antibodies seek out and bond to body muscle tissue. Each doom unit has a radioactive isotope (Bismuth-212) attached to the antibody "vehicle."

Bismuth-212 decays by alpha radiation, the emission of alpha particles (helium nuclei). The energy of alpha particles is high enough to kill any cell it passes through and has a penetration level of approximately ten cells. Doom destroys the surface layers of muscle tissue. As soon as the dead tissue has been removed by the body's own waste-disposal system, doom proceeds to attack and destroy the layers underneath. This will, theoretically, continue until there is no muscle left, but in most affected creatures death usually occurs before that can happen.

Once introduced into the body, and until it is destroyed and removed, doom removes one box from the subject's maximum Physical and Mental Condition Monitors. (After two days a subject may sustain only a maximum of eight boxes of physical and eight boxes of mental damage instead of the regular ten each.) Furthermore, every two days, doom permanently removes 1 point from the character's Body Rating, and one from his Strength Rating. Death occurs when the individual's Body or Strength Rating falls to 0, when his condition monitor is reduced to 0, or if damage through trauma exceeds the new maximum condition rating.

Doom is difficult to treat. Binder does not recognize doom as a toxin, and antibac and z-interferon are equally useless because doom is neither a bacteria nor a virus. Cybernetic blood filters and biological pathogenic defense systems do offer some assistance in combating doom, but only operate at half-effectiveness (round up). Although doom inflicts no conventional damage, doom resists as if having a damage code of 6M2.

Diagnosing and identifying doom is a relatively simple task (especially if done with a radiation meter); two or more successes on a Biotech (5) Test (or Biotech (3) Test if using a radiation meter) indicate correct analysis. A cleansing gene therapy procedure can stop the continuing effects of doom, though any attribute damage already done is permanent.

Rating	Speed	Vectors	Price
"6M2"	Special	Air and contact	500¥/dose

>>>>>[If this is the kind of drek floating around after the ban on microbiologicals came down, I don't even want to think about what was circulating before.]<<<<<
—Rapid Fire <14:53:24/12-21-52>

>>>>>[A lot of the stuff went "missing" while the ban was being legislated into operation. It's probably still out there—somewhere.]<<<<<
—The Smiling Bandit <Strikes again!/Ha-Ha-Ha>

>>>>>[Thanks mucho for telling me. I feel so much safer now.]<<<<<
—Rapid Fire <17:01:45/12-21-52>

GAMMA-ANTHRAX

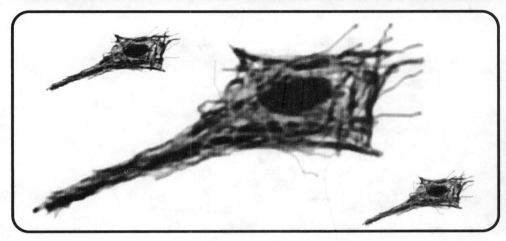

ORDER HERE

RATINGS

Legality Rating: **2-M3**

Availability: **14/30 days**

Street Index: **6**

Gamma-anthrax is a mutated strain of the already deadly anthracosis bacillus, and is lethal if left untreated. Gamma-anthrax delivers an initial damage of 6S2 Stun upon exposure; this damage was engineered into the disease in order to disguise the bacterial agent as a lesser toxin and hide its true nature. Its incubation period is variable, depending on the character's health and physique. Make a Body Success Test against g-anthrax's rating of 6S2; the number of successes indicate the incubation period in days.

After incubation, g-anthrax manifests as cold-like symptoms, becoming a fulminating pneumonia as the disease progresses. Once the disease takes hold, the character begins to weaken. Remove two boxes from the maximum of both his Physical and Mental Condition Monitors every 12 hours the disease progresses beyond its incubation stage (i.e., after 24 hours the individual may sustain only a maximum of six boxes of either physical or mental damage instead of the regular ten). Death occurs if the monitors are brought to 0 or if damage to the character exceeds the monitor's new maximum through external means such as combat. In addition, every day the disease manifests, add +1 to the bacteria's Strength for purposes of resisting any treatments (after two days, g-anthrax's Resistance Code is effectively 8S2) and apply a +1 to the target numbers for all tests made by the subject. Gamma-anthrax may be delivered by aerosol, contact, or injection.

Unlike regular anthrax, the gamma strain is non-infectious. Both, however, are potentially deadly if medical attention is not administered promptly. If treatments are successful, recovery from g-anthrax infection is relatively simple, and proceeds as if the subject had received wounds corresponding to the number of boxes removed from the condition monitors. (For example, if the individual had five boxes removed from his/her maximum, recovery proceeds as if he/she had suffered five boxes of physical and five boxes of mental damage.)

To accurately diagnose g-anthrax, make a Biotech (6) Test. Laboratory conditions, or lack thereof, may increase or decrease the Target Number. The Target Number with a good lab is 5, for a poor lab or no lab, it is 8.

0 successes = No result/Inconclusive
1 = Bacteriological agent present
2–3 = Bacillus type, probably lethal
4+ = Any relevant data, including treatment.

Additional Biotech Tests may be made every hour if initial results fail to deliver acceptable results, but only if further tests are conducted.

Rating	Speed	Vectors	Price
6S2 Stun	Varies	Air, contact, and injection	180¥/dose

>>>>>[Story is that the contaminated belt in southern Africa is the result of one country's attempt to keep its rebels under control using this stuff. The popular version of the tale has it that government troops hadn't anticipated the effects of the favorable climate. The conditions let the bacteria propagate and spread like wildfire.]<<<<<
　　—Tango <21:36:14/12-21-52>

>>>>>[No matter what the real story, fact remains that this incident was another reason why the unilateral ban was established back in '41.]<<<<<
　　—Fastjack <23:08:57/12-21-52>

ORDER HERE

RATINGS

Legality Rating: **Legal**

Availability: **Always**

Street Index: **1**

MYCO-PROTEIN

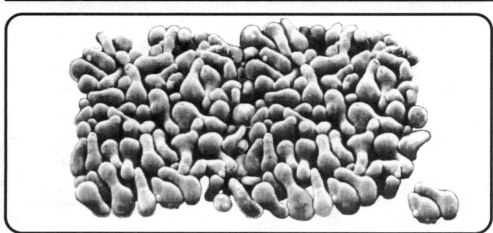

With the start of the Resource Rush more than 40 years ago, much of the world's arable land fell prey to exploitation of a different, much harsher sort. Loss of such fertile soil to industrial development put heavy pressure on the remaining arable land to produce far beyond its capabilities. The inability to meet the demands for food production on a global scale has driven food prices to their highest level ever, and has created a market for cheaper alternate sources of consumable products. Today, most available food comes from products derived from single-cell proteins.

The consumption of microorganisms for their food value is nothing new. People have eaten them in one form or another (yeast in leavened bread, lactic acid bacteria in cheese, molds in fermented sausage, and so on) since ancient times. Modern techniques for incorporating these organisms into the human diet originated in Great Britain in 1879 with the introduction of *Saccharomyces cerevisiae*, or baker's yeast. In Germany during World War II, *Candida utilis* (torula yeast) was cultured as a protein source for humans and animals, using sulphite waste liquor (from pulp and paper manufacture) and wood sugar as its raw materials. Although several microorganisms can provide an adequate source of food energy, present-day production of "food-substitutes" for humans centers almost exclusively on mold and fungi platforms.

Growth rates of mold and higher fungi (4 to 16 hours) are slower than those for bacteria and yeast (2 to 3 hours), but mold and fungi are a greater source of protein (72 percent by weight, as opposed to 35 percent). Cultured in aerated fermenters, and using glucose as raw material, *Fusarium graminearum* has a generation time of 5.5 hours and yields .8 kilograms dry weight of cells for every kilogram of sugar consumed. Once harvested, the collected cells are then treated to reduce ribonucleic acid content (consumption of more than 2 grams of untreated ribonucleic acid per day by humans may cause kidney stones or gout). The filamentous mycelium cakes can then be flavored, formed, and textured into products resembling anything desired by the consumer (chicken, beef, pork, and so forth).

Price
25¥/kilogram

>>>>>[You know, in all my 29 years, I've never had a real steak.]<<<<<
—Neon Samurai <09:15:26/12-22-52>

>>>>>[Meat is overrated. Fruit, on the other hand...You haven't lived until you've tasted real, fresh fruit.]<<<<<
—Feral <11:25:31/12-22-52>

>>>>>[Drek, I'd be happy to know I was eating every night.]<<<<<
—Digger <12:47:05/12-22-52>

CHEMISTRY

"Sticks and stones may break your bones, but drugs will really fry you."
—Inner city graffiti

"Drugs! Drugs! Drugs! Why is everybody so preoccupied with drugs? I'm just a law-abiding chemical industrialist. Why should I know anything about drugs?"
—Abraham Costa, "Industrialist," testifying before UCAS Supreme Court

Chemistry is the study of matter. It deals with matter's composition and properties, its reactions with other forms of matter, and the application of the derived knowledge to a specific subject or activity. Understanding the principles of chemistry gives a chemist much the same ability as giving a pencil and a sketchbook to an artist—the ability to create.

Being able to create, control, and manipulate matter makes possible many things. The quality of life that most of us take for granted, for instance, would never have reached present levels without the help of chemical technology.

In the modern world, chemistry is the "Everyman" technology—the great equalizer. Chemical technology is inexpensive, readily available, and does not require a great deal of "personal" time or investment. There's a chemical for every occasion, and if there is no off-the-shelf chemical that fits someone's requirements, that person can always get one designed.

APPLIED INDUSTRIAL CHEMISTRY

In discussing the science of chemistry for use in **Shadowrun**, it is necessary to differentiate the application of chemistry into the functional delineations: industrial and pharmaceutical. Pharmaceutical chemistry deals with medicines and compounds that affect body chemistry, and industrial chemistry deals with everything else.

Chemistry is a "feedback" science. It advances in directions dictated by the current needs of the society it serves. **Shadowrun** society is very much corporate-centric, and the corporations themselves are built around a heavy commercial base.

Commerce, to put it most simply, consists of the buying, selling, and trading of goods and services. These goods must somehow be manufactured, and most manufacturing processes involve a great deal of chemistry. This chemistry may involve processes as minor as determining what kind of lubricant to use in the machinery, or may, in fact, be the actual product itself.

OPTICAL CHIPS

One chemically based industry that dominates a large share of the world market is the production of optical chips. Optical technology (especially in the form of chips and switches) is essential for many of the aspects of modern day-to-day life. The sale of devices based largely on optical technology is a multi-billion nuyen industry, and accounts for a staggering 43 percent of Japan's exports and for 26 percent of overall world trade.

The most widely sold product of optical technology is the optical memory chip. At the heart of optical memory technology is an organic pigment known as bacteriorhodopsin (part of the photosynthetic system of the bacterium *halobacterium halobium*). Bacteriorhodopsin exists physically in two states: one that absorbs green light and one that absorbs red light. In

>>>>>[Every good urban guerrilla or runner wannabe should invest some time and effort in the study of chemistry. Beside having achieved the lofty height of expanding his intellectual horizons, a master of chemistry is never without a weapon—or a steady supply of homegrown explosives.]<<<<<
—Feral <17:38:19/12-22-52>

>>>>>[Not to disagree with my esteemed colleague, but chemistry is more than the art of cooking plastique. Chemistry can be applied in a much more subtle fashion—even on a run.
Try using a dart pistol or a "squirt" gun loaded with narcojet rounds or shocktox next time you face off with some of the corporate competition. In some cases, that stuff is even more effective than regular bullets, and it definitely changes the other guy's attitude when he knows you're not out trying to send him to an early grave.
How about some acid instead of C4 on those locks? A bit slow, granted, but using it won't announce your presence to the

its green-absorbing state, the bacteriorhodopsin molecule's electronic configuration changes to become red-absorbing, and vice versa. This two-state (binary) characteristic is what makes the pigment useful as a memory-storage medium.

By using lasers of differing wavelengths (specifically attuned to the red and green frequencies of light), information can be stored in and retrieved from bacteriorhodopsin molecules in much the same way as with magnetic memory, in the form of on/off sequences. The similarities in the physical properties of optical and electromagnetic media end with their shared binary nature, however. Individual clusters of bacteriorhodopsin are much smaller than magnetic sites, allowing for the creation of optical chips with more storage sites than a solid state or magnetic component of the same surface area. Once its configuration has been set,

bacteriorhodopsin is much more stable than its electromagnetic counterpart. Shifts in environmental variables (high magnetic fields, temperature changes, shock, and so on) will not affect its physical state. Only a pulse of light at the right wavelength can change the molecule's properties. The cycle time of the optical pigment is less than five-trillionths of a second, making bacteriorhodopsin-based optical storage more than a thousand times faster than conventional magnetic memory.

When scanned by a low-power laser, the absorption feature can also function as an optical gate or switch. If the laser is trained on an oppositely colored cluster and cannot provide the molecule with the level of energy necessary to change the pigment's current configuration, the molecule will simply block the beam from continuing on its path. If trained on a similarly colored cluster, the low-power beam will pass through, unimpeded in its progress. In this way, individual clusters operate as high-speed polarizing gates for optical microcircuitry.

Combining the storage and switching functions of bacteriorhodopsin within a single unit allows for the construction of highly sophisticated integrated packages much like the silicon-based chip designs using semiconductor chemistry—only smaller and faster.

SUPERCONDUCTORS

The first observed and most distinctive property of a superconductive body is the near total loss of electrical resistance at a critical temperature (each specific material has its own unique threshold point). Peripheral and secondary characteristics include the levitation and suspension effects that accompany superconductivity. It is for the null-resistance property that superconductive materials are most prized.

When electrical energy passes through standard conductive material, a percentage of the transmitted energy is lost in overcoming the substance's natural resistance to the current. This resistance, though small, can account for massive amounts of power (and therefore money) lost when dealing with large voltages and currents, such as those in power transmission lines, large electric motors, and so on. The use of superconductive materials virtually eliminates the problem. Even low-voltage and low-current systems benefit from negated resistance (e.g., clearer signals on wire transmissions, improved reception from antennas, longer use from battery-based equipment, and such). The low resistance of superconductors also alleviates many of the temperature problems caused by standard electronics. In standard equipment, an individual component's

occupants of the entire compound. Drek, if you're in such a fraggin' rush, use thermite—slow thermite. The thermite reaction will create enough heat to melt through most locking systems in about a second.

With the proper attitude and equipment, you can be in and out of a complex without firing a single bullet.]<<<<<
—The Smiling Bandit <Strikes again!/Ha-Ha-Ha>

>>>>>[Well drek. That's no fun.]<<<<<
—Feral <09:16:00/12-23-52>

>>>>>[Stay alive first. Have fun second. You can't party when you're dead.]<<<<<
—Winger <10:07:45/12-23-52>

>>>>>[A good run is one where you get in, grab the stuff you came for, and leave without anyone being the wiser. You've blown it if you

resistance can build up the unit's heat level to an operating temperature beyond its rated limits, causing component failure. Components constructed from superconducting materials have virtually no resistance and therefore generate almost no heat; because they cannot suffer breakdown due to high internal heat, superconducting electronics can be run faster and with a far greater load on their components.

A strange by-product of the superconductive phenomenon is the Schwartz effect (better known as the suspension effect). The basic result of the Schwartz effect is that superconductors can cause magnetized objects to levitate above them. A variation on the effect is that a magnetized object can cause a superconductor to be suspended in space under it. An example of this is the near-frictionless, energy-efficient, levitating/suspended, high-speed mass transit system.

Although still hotly debated after more than 50 years, the Goddard theorem has become the de facto definition behind the superconductivity phenomenon. Essentially, the theory explains that certain elements within superconductive compounds force some of the component oxygen atoms to lose a single electron and develop a spin. This spinning causes the atoms on either side of the oxygen atoms to line up in the same direction, creating pockets of magnetism. The oxygen atoms that have been deprived of electrons act as "holes," attracting electrons from other nearby oxygen atoms, which, in turn, lose their electrons and thus form new holes. These holes moving in sequential patterns create trails of magnetic pockets that facilitate the flow of electrons. This smooth flow of electrons represents superconductivity.

The Goddard theorem precludes superconductivity at room temperature. However, certain families of superconducting alloys have high enough threshold temperatures that standard refrigerants can be used to achieve the material's superconductive state. Bismuth compounds have critical temperatures hovering around $-163°$ C., while thallium alloys achieve superconductivity as high as $-148°$ C. Either liquid oxygen ($-182.9°$ C.) or liquid nitrogen ($-195.8°$ C.) can be used to refrigerate these potential superconductors to well bellow their critical points.

While the problems of maintaining critical temperatures with refrigeration systems hamper the application of superconductive materials on a grand scale, superconductors can still play a surprisingly large number of roles within today's technology. The search continues, however, for disproof of the Goddard theorem and the ever-elusive room-temperature superconductor.

PHARMACEUTICALS

In the modern vocabulary there has developed a moral and ethical gap between the concepts of "medicine" and "drugs." The term medicine is used to refer to a chemical of beneficial nature and effect, while the term drug is assigned to compounds used primarily in self-indulgence and self-destruction. The difference between a medicine and a poison is mostly only a matter of dosage. When used in low concentrations, many poisons are useful in treating certain conditions, and any medicine can become toxic when administered in excess. In fact, anything can become toxic if taken in extreme amounts, even water and oxygen.

Pharmaceuticals work by acting on receptors, specialized proteins that form part of the surface membrane of cells. This action varies with each chemical and includes stimulating, reducing, inhibiting, and initiating. Pharmaceutical chemicals may be further differentiated into the following categories: stimulants, depressants/tranquilizers, hallucinogens/psychedelics, and utility compounds (a catchall category for everything that does not fit into one of the preceding classifications). All medicines and drugs fall under one of these headings (and some fall under more than one), the important factor being the degree and level of chemical action.

STIMULANTS

A stimulant may be broadly defined as any substance that quickens the rate of physical or mental activity. Stimulants vary from broad-spectrum (adrenalin) to specific, narrow-focused types (digitalis, which stimulates the heart muscles, or diuretics, which stimulate action in the kidneys). For a stimulant to be effective, there must be a certain amount of reserve energy in the organ to be stimulated. To use a stimulant in the absence of such a reserve is akin to whipping an exhausted horse.

The overuse of stimulants leads to massive overexhaustion as the body exerts itself to the point where all its reserves are drained and depleted. Further use of stimulants at this point invites death and accomplishes little else. If an additional dose of a stimulant is administered before the effects of the first application have worn off, or before the subject has recovered from using up his bodily reserves, he/she takes an immediate Light wound on the Mental Condition Monitor. Moreover, the additional application (and any subsequent doses) operates at only 50 percent efficiency. Divide bonuses in half, rounding down; penalties are not correspondingly altered.

have to draw your gun and shoot your way out. Survival depends on forethought and planning, not on who's a better shot.]<<<<<
—Tango <12:43:26/12-23-52>

>>>>>[There are times when you have no choice, however; times when you have to get past security in order to reach your objective.]<<<<<
—The Neon Samurai <13:11:51/12-23-52>

>>>>>[Yeah! Now those are my kinda runs. Man, I love the smell of cordite.]<<<<<
—Feral <15:29:34/12-23-52>

>>>>>[Figures.]<<<<<
—Winger <18:24:52/12-23-52>

Stimulants are an example of chemical technology being used to equalize the odds at very little monetary expense. Many smaller companies (and some larger corporations) do not have the resources (or won't spend the money) to equip and train a large security force. As an alternative, several such firms have turned to using tailored amphetamines to give their men the extra edge to keep them competitive with their cybernetically enhanced and/or biologically augmented opponents. It is a matter of simple economy. How much more economical to throw hordes of "pumped-up" men (doped up at very little financial cost) at a problem, than to arm each individual security guard in compensating bioware/cyberware (costing thousands of nuyen per person), even taking into consideration the high casualty figures of actual unit confrontation. Though the drawbacks inherent in repeated use of such stimulants are widely known, there has never been a shortage of volunteers (both real and forced). There are just not enough jobs to go around in the first place. For the companies involved, it is a cost-effective and adequate, though not quite ethical or moral, solution to their problems. And very few guards employed in this fashion last long enough to apply for the medical severance made available by their employers.

TRANQUILIZERS

Tranquilizers are chemicals that reduce mental and physical activity. In modern vernacular, however, they have become identified with their effects on a subject's mental state. In that respect, a tranquilizer ideally becomes a drug capable of allaying tension, worry, anxiety, and panic, without impairing the normal mental capacity of a given individual. This is rarely the case, however. Although tranquilizers are physically and chemically able to perform their functions, the mental fallout from the effects of such blissful calm, restfulness, and pleasure quickly fosters the strong desire to experience such states at all times.

Tranquilizing drugs exist in a wide range of strength and effects, including narcotics, sedatives, hypnotics, and tranquilizers. A sedative reduces overactivity of the nervous system (diminishing excitement and irritability), hypnotics aim to produce sleep, and tranquilizers attempt to quell states of mental stress. Narcotics fall on the borderline between sedatives and hypnotics, relieving pain while inducing sleep.

The results of substance-abuse research show tranquilizing-type drugs as the most commonly encountered group of misused chemicals, far more even than hallucinogens.

Part of the problem with tranquilizer misuse stems from their relatively low purchase price and wide availability. Barbiturates, for example, are sold on the street at less than 40¥ a "hit." Another problem far more difficult to correct arises from society itself. For individuals who have fallen through the cracks in the system, there is very little hope. Many turn to tranquilizer use to alleviate the depression accompanying their situation.

On the corporate side, tranquilizers of some form or another are often the first physical line of defense. If individuals manage to penetrate a corporate complex's perimeter defenses, it is simpler, far more cost-effective, and much more efficient to remove the threat by neutralizing the invader with chemical tranquilizers than by mobilizing a security team and risking employee injury or loss and property damage.

HALLUCINOGENS

These chemicals alter the mental and emotional processes of their users, producing visual and/or auditory hallucinations. Although they have been used throughout history as mind- and sensory-enhancing drugs, they are potentially the most dangerous of all drugs. The nature of their chemical action promotes high instances of neural and brain disorders stemming from their use. Many hallucinogenic drugs carry additional side effects, psychotomimetic action being among the most distressing. Psychotomimetic drugs stimulate mental illness, eventually causing permanent mental trauma, brain dysfunction, and neurosis. Several hallucinogenic compounds such as Ecstasy and Zen are, unfortunately, available on the street. With hallucinogens ranging from 80¥ to 120¥ a dose, however, they are relatively expensive when compared to other available drugs. That is the main reason they are rarely chosen over the less-expensive tranquilizing compounds or the repeat-use BTL chip.

Hallucinogens and psychedelics are commonly referred to as "escapist" drugs, allowing the user to flee into a world of sensory splendor. In actuality, they are deadly substances, letting their advocates "escape" only into neurological oblivion.

Despite the dangers involved with their use, hallucinogens have applications where the user's continued health is not a primary concern. Because of the disorienting nature of hallucinogens and psychedelics, several unscrupulous organizations and individuals have found them useful as truth drugs and interrogation compounds.

>>>>>[With all those side effects, using drugs is like taking on the entire Metroplex Guard with a BB gun. Not very smart and ultimately terminal.]<<<<<
—Digger <20:22:04/12-23-52>

>>>>>[Actually, many of these "problem" pharmaceutical compounds exist in several distinct chemical algorithms. That is, they have the same composition, but are arranged in a different physical shape.
Often, one of the compound's stereoisomers is a completely safe derivative with none of the harmful side effects usually associated with the drug. It's been proven that thalidomide(-), for example, is entirely free of any ill effects.]<<<<<
—The Smiling Bandit <Strikes again!/Ha-Ha-Ha>

SUBSTANCE USE/ABUSE

All drugs have an Addiction Rating, a Tolerance Rating, and a Strength Rating. Together, these three attributes define the compound's Danger Profile.

Addiction to a substance may be either physical (P) or mental (M). Mental dependence usually stems from the emotional gratification derived from use of a drug. Tests for mental addiction are made against the drug-user's Willpower Attribute. Physical addiction is a much "harder" addiction and results from the body becoming dependent on the presence of the used substance for its continued "survival." The damage done to the subject's metabolism makes such a condition much more difficult to overcome. Tests for physical dependence are made against the drug-user's Body Attribute. To determine whether or not a subject becomes addicted to a compound, make a standard Resistance Test using the drug's Addiction Rating as a Target Number against the appropriate attribute. It takes only one success to remain unaddicted (if the substance is both physically and mentally addictive, make a separate test for each one). If the test fails, the character becomes addicted to the substance.

Once addicted, he or she requires at least one dose of the substance every Body x 4 hours for physical addictions and every Willpower x 4 hours for mental dependencies. The period between doses may be extended only once by an additional Body/Willpower number of hours; this is accomplished by making a successful Body/Willpower Test against the current Addiction Rating. Failing to acquire and administer a dose in the required time results in the character going into immediate withdrawal. Dosages required by the addict begin to increase, as the addict desires more and more of the substance in question (eventually hitting a toxic level, which varies from drug to drug). In addition to experiencing substance cravings, a character who is addicted loses one-half point of Essence (a permanent loss) and one box from both his Physical and Mental Condition Monitors (starting from the top and working down) for every week he remains addicted. The user will eventually die when his Essence reaches 0 or if damage to his Condition Monitor(s) exceeds his new maximum. That is, after two weeks of substance addiction, a character will have lost 1 point of Essence, and have a maximum physical and mental condition of only eight boxes instead of the regular ten.

Tolerance is a measure of how easy it is to become "immunized" to the effects of the chemical. To determine acquired immunity, make a Body Resistance Test against a Target Number equal to the drug's Tolerance Rating. If the character fails to roll any successes in this test, he has become permanently immune to the substance's effect. Individuals who undergo certain "cleansing" forms of gene therapy lose this tolerance in the process and may use the drug once again if they wish. Characters who are addicted and who acquire immunity go into immediate withdrawal.

The tests to determine Tolerance and Addiction are made after the drug has been administered and its effects have worn off.

The drug's Strength Rating indicates the ease with which dependency and immunity are acquired in the long-term use of the drug. Every time the number of applications taken/administered equals a multiple of the compound's Strength Rating, add +1 to both the Addiction and Tolerance Rating. For example, if the drug's Strength Rating is 5, every fifth dose adds +1 to both the drug's Addiction and Tolerance Ratings. The new ratings become the drug's Addiction and Tolerance Ratings for that particular character, and further use by the character will continue to increase these ratings. Given enough time, Addiction and Tolerance Ratings will drop, but never below their "base" ratings. Every 30 minus the drug's Strength days of uninterrupted non-drug use (for that particular drug), Addiction and Tolerance Ratings are reduced by 1. This period is the drug's "clean period."

At some point, an addicted character may wish to "kick the habit." To quit an addiction is difficult and the effort can begin only after the character makes a successful Willpower Test against the addictive substance's current Addiction Rating + 1. This roll may be modified by mitigating external circumstances, such as strong peer support, a long stay at the New Betty Ford clinic, and so on. For a physical addiction, roll against the current Addiction Rating + 3. If the subject has both a mental and a physical dependency to the drug, the Target Number increases to the current Addiction Rating + 4. Only if all the tests succeed may the character continue with the recovery process (remember that successes may be purchased with earned Karma). Addiction recovery attempts may only be made if the gamemaster feels that they are warranted (a player may not decide that his character is cured without cause). A character may deal with only one substance at a time.

During the recovery process, all losses from substance abuse are temporarily halted, but not removed. In addition, the individual suffers a +2 to all his target numbers (+4 for concen-

>>>>>[Be that as it may, but none of these "safe" derivatives are commonly available, nor are they inexpensive. Not many people will bother going to the trouble or expense to find them.]<<<<<
—Fastjack <08:01:53/12-24-52>

>>>>>[Even acknowledging the existence of derivatives that are physically "safe," much of the danger in substance abuse still lies in the chemical's effect on the user's psyche and mental state.]<<<<<
—KAM <08:54:12/12-24-52>

>>>>>[Stereoisomers, derivatives, subject's psyche—what drek! I've lived all my life on the streets and I've seen and heard every excuse for drug use there is: "It's the only way to compete," "Life's too painful," "I'm in complete control," ,"It's safe and I'm only an occasional user"…All of it's not worth a fraggin' thimble of barghest piss in the end.

tration tasks, including spellcasting). This is because of the combined ordeal of withdrawal pains and mental/physical shock. The penalties and effects of withdrawal vanish immediately if a dose of the "required" drug is administered. In that case, however, the recovering character is automatically considered addicted once again, and the drug's current Addiction Rating increases +1. If the character has the strength and courage to weather the recovery process, the drug's Addiction Rating drops 1 point every three days. Once the rating drops to its base level (it may never drop below its starting level), the character is no longer addicted to the particular substance. At this point, Essence loss is "permanently" halted, but lost Essence can never be regained. The subject must then rest an additional length of time equal to the drug's Addiction Rating in order to restore his physical and mental health. During this time, his shock penalties drop to +1 for all his target numbers (+2 for concentration-based activities). The character recovers the damage on his Condition Monitors at a rate of one physical

and one mental box every three days of rest; once the rest cycle has elapsed, all performance penalties are removed. The character must rest for the full period in order to eliminate the penalties and restore his mental/physical health. Only at the end of this process is he fully "cured."

Alternately, in other circumstances (e.g., the character cannot obtain the addictive drug on time), a character may suffer forced withdrawal. This is not a recovery process, but a failure to satisfy artificially induced substance cravings. Losses due to addiction continue to accrue throughout a forced withdrawal period. During forced withdrawal, the character may feel physically and emotionally almost worse than death. All his target numbers suffer a +3 performance penalty (+6 to Concentration skills, including spellcasting). Also, the individual is in a state of constant pain and will behave as if suffering from the effects of a persistent Moderate mental wound. This status is his/her minimum Damage Level while undergoing forced withdrawal; apply appropriate damage penalties to Initiative and target numbers, in addition to the withdrawal penalties. The effects and penalties associated with the withdrawal process are immediately removed once a dose of the "required" drug is administered. However, easing away the trauma of forced withdrawal by taking in the abused drug only reinforces the addiction; the drug's current Addiction Rating immediately increases +1. Characters undergoing forced withdrawal will do just about anything to get a "hit" of their desired substance. If a period of 24 hours passes without the character receiving a dose, the drug's current Addiction Rating drops by 1 point (but never lower than its starting base). The individual is still considered addicted, however, and will continue to experience forced withdrawal until he/she is administered a dose.

Magic cannot be used to aid directly in recovering from substance addiction (as such dependency is not, technically, either a toxin, a disease, or a wound). A spell such as Resist Moderate Pain can alleviate the pain associated with forced withdrawal, however. Similarly, the character may undertake certain cleansing therapies (if he has the necessary resources and can locate the facilities) to remove physical addictions (and return lost mental and physical condition boxes), although these can provide no assistance in recovering from mental dependencies. The body may no longer need the drug, but the mind still craves its presence.

Drug addiction is a very debilitating experience. The best solution is prevention—not to become dependent in the first place.

Given a choice, I'd rather put a gun to my head and pull the trigger. It's faster, less painful, and has a lot more dignity involved.]<<<<<
    —Digger <10:38:14/12-24-52>

>>>>>[Old man Running Cloud never works any magic without first taking a hit of Zen. He says it expands the reach of his mind and gives him added strength.]<<<<<
    —Rapid Fire <13:27:00/12-24-52>

>>>>>[Yeah? Well there's a reason why we in the magic biz call him *Crazy* Cloud. It's questionable these days whether or not any kind of narcotic or hallucinogen is needed for the Art.]<<<<<
    —MLC III <16:05:39/12-24-52>

COMPOUNDS

"Better living through chemistry—that's what I always say."
— D. I. Greig, Entrepreneur

"If you can call it living! You ever see what this stuff does to you?"
—Mark Ferguson, Officer, Metroplex 23 Division

"Whaddya think I am? Crazy? I don't use it...just sell it."
—D. I. Greig, Entrepreneur

Science is, among other things, a tool. In itself it is neither right nor wrong, good nor bad. And yet it can be any of these things, depending on whose hand wields the technology.

Chemistry, like genetics, is a field of science with vast potential. Elemental in nature, chemistry affects the basic "stuff" of physical creation, making it a force of nature that can be channeled by man.

Manmade compounds can be creative or destructive, protective or threatening, healing or destroying. From among the countless compounds in existence, **Shadowtech** presents only a minute fraction, but this fraction is representative of chemistry's potentials to build, heal, protect, and destroy.

>>>>>[Looks like it's time to break out the 'ol credstick and go shopping again.]<<<<<
   —Winger <16:46:17/12-26-52>

>>>>>[You know, I practically live in the malls already.]<<<<<
   —Tim <18:10:32/12-26-52>

>>>>>[Hate to tell you this, Tim, but you do live in a mall—in the ventilation ducts.]<<<<<
   —Digger <22:57:28/12-26-52>

ORDER HERE

RATINGS

Legality Rating: **Legal**

Availability: **4/10 days**

Street Index: **2**

CARCERANDS

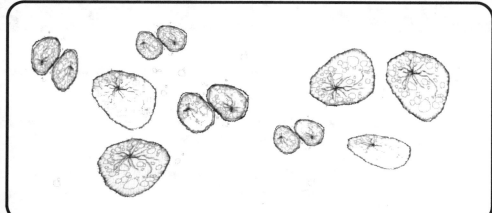

Carcerands are molecular bodies whose structures resemble empty spheres. They are made by combining two cavitands (a cavity containing bowl-shaped ring molecules). When two cavitands are brought together in a solution, they trap small amounts of the solution as they combine to form a carcerand.

Carcerands are used to release chemicals into an organism over a period of time. Degradation of individual carcerands by the acids and enzymes within the target organism slowly release the trapped compound into the organism's body. Depending on its exact composition, a carcerand may degrade as quickly as one hour or as slowly as up to one year after introduction into the organism's system.

Delay	Price
1 hour	25¥ x Agent cost
12 hours	50¥ x Agent cost
24 hours	100¥ x Agent cost
1 week	200¥ x Agent cost
2 weeks	400¥ x Agent cost
1 month	800¥ x Agent cost
2 months	1,600¥ x Agent cost
6 months	3,200¥ x Agent cost
1 year	6,400¥ x Agent cost

>>>>>[With careful logistical planning, carcerands can be a real ace up the sleeve.]<<<<<
—Tango <06:33:21/12-27-52>

>>>>>[But it's mostly certain megacorps who use them as persuasion devices. "We've just injected you with 'fill in the blank'. In just 24 hours you'll be a corpse unless you get the antidote—and we're the only ones who've got it. Sure, we'll give it to you, but first there's something we want you to do for us…"). You get the idea.]<<<<<
—The Neon Samurai <08:54:19/12-27-52>

DIKOTE™

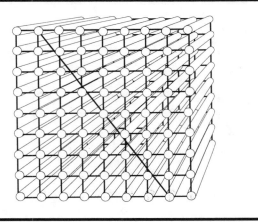

ORDER HERE

RATINGS

Legality Rating: **Legal**

Availability: **6/14 days**

Street Index: **10**

Dikote™ is a process that deposits a thin diamond film on any solid surface. Small volumes of methane gas are mixed with large volumes of hydrogen gas, then subjected to powerful beams of microwave energy. This creates a plasma, a super-hot gas in which all atoms are ionized. The plasma is then passed over the cooler solid target, forming a diamond film as the gases condense on the surface.

The diamond film imparts much more structural strength and resilience to conventional materials, adding +2 to the Structural/Barrier Rating, and +1 to any ballistic and +1 to any impact armor present. When Dikote is used to coat a melee weapon, the Strength Rating for an attack made with the treated weapon increases by +1 (e.g., 5M2 becomes 6M2). If applied to an edged instrument the weapon's potential wounding increases by one level. A sword's normal Damage Code is (Str)M2, for example, but a sword with Dikote inflicts damage and is resisted as if it were (Str)S2. A similarly treated projectile weapon has the effective Strength of the thrower raised by +1. Parrying with a Dikote-treated object adds an additional die for defensive purposes only.

Treated products also find use in the construction of high-speed bearings. Bearings treated with Dikote™ last in high-temperature environments where conventional lubricants break down, permitting the development of faster, more efficient, more powerful engines and turbines.

Application of Dikote technology has also benefited the electronics industry. Conventional silicon chips generate large amounts of heat while operating, which requires that individual components be relatively far apart to prevent overheating. As the diamond film sheds more heat much faster than silicon, electronic components layered on a Dikote film may be packed in denser formations (resulting in smaller and lighter products) and can also function in such super-hot environments as jet engines or nuclear reactors, where silicon would fail regularly. Diamond film semiconductors can also withstand higher voltages, permitting their use in various facets of microwave communication technology. In contrast to silicon, which will not function for a period of days to weeks after exposure to radiation, Dikote components will also continue operating after such exposure.

A Dikote-treated jacket contains roughly 1.5m² of material, a full suit 2.25m², and a long coat 2.75m² meters.

Edged weapons with Dikote can inflict damage against "hardened" (i.e., vehicular) targets. When so used, these weapons reduce their normal (unmodified) Damage Code by one level. Against a man, a glazed sword, for example, would be (Str)S2; against a car, the same sword would be (Str)M2.

Price
1,000¥/100 cm² (1,000¥ minimum)

>>>>>[Not everything can be glazed with Dikote. The item treated must be able to withstand the heat generated by the plasma. This obviously eliminates cloth and plastic, which, unfortunately, comprise the bulk of casual armor these days. If you've got some of the heavier stuff or ceramic armor, getting it glazed is a great idea. If you have the money.]<<<<<
    —The Smiling Bandit <Strikes again!/Ha-Ha-Ha>

>>>>>[I've seen a Dikote-treated sword in action. That thing sliced clear through anything in its way!]<<<<<
    —The Neon Samurai <11:21:00/12-27-52>

>>>>>[I've heard the stuff wears off in about six months or so, but…maybe it depends on what you hit and how often you hit it.]<<<<<
    —Hatchetman <11:43:45/12-27-52>

ORDER HERE

RATINGS

Legality Rating: **Legal**

Availability: **2/12 hours**

Street Index: **1.5**

DMSO

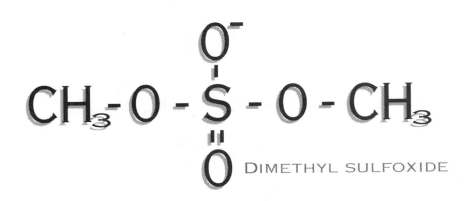

$$CH_3 - O - \overset{\overset{\displaystyle O^-}{\|}}{\underset{\underset{\displaystyle O}{\|}}{S}} - O - CH_3$$

DIMETHYL SULFOXIDE

Though dimethyl sulfoxide (DMSO) is a utility chemical with a number of applications, its most common use is as a carrier that forces the skin to absorb delivered chemicals. DMSO is soluble in acetone, alcohol, ether, and water; it is liquid at room temperature and is non-reactive with most other compounds. Upon contact with skin, DMSO, and whatever else is dissolved in solution with it, is instantly absorbed into the body. DMSO is used to deliver many chemical and biological agents.

Porous armor (such as armor clothing and Kevlar™ weaves) offers no protection against DMSO. Any attack successes not negated by a Dodge Test indicate "flesh" contact, and will allow the "carried" solution to enter and affect the body. Rigid armor (higher than 5, or plated) applies half its Defensive Rating (rounded up) against DMSO attacks (some attacks penetrate at the articulation points). Only individuals in fully sealed rigid armor or in protective suits specifically designed to protect against chemical/biological agents are immune to the penetrating effect of DMSO.

Price
10¥ + Agent cost/unit

ARES SQUIRT

For all those times you want to keep the shooting friendly, Ares Arms introduces the squirt. Load up the bottom reservoir with the special gel (250¥ per refill), lock in a vial of your favorite chemical rounds, and you're ready to go. Armored targets don't present a problem. With Ares' patented DMSO gelling agent, a solid hit is all that is needed. Accuracy is another added feature. The gel's in-air shot stability offers superb accuracy even at extended ranges.

Best of all, the squirt uses compressed air, which makes it completely silent and totally recoilless.

Type	Concealment	Ammo	Damage	Weight	Price
Light	7	10/20* (cartridge)	Special	1.75	750¥

*Chemical cartridge holds 10 shots, gel reservoir holds enough for 20 shots (reservoir must be reloaded once for every 2 cartridge reloads).

>>>>>[Be careful handling this stuff; spilling some on yourself can be bad—even if it's straight DMSO and not some mixed concoction. If the DMSO touches, or is applied to, a skin area with dirt or other contaminants, whatever's there goes straight into the bloodstream. Sometimes that can make you quite sick.]<<<<<
—The Smiling Bandit <Strikes again!/Ha-Ha-Ha>

>>>>>[Not all things can be delivered by a DMSO vehicle. DMSO works by causing the molecular "gates" within the walls of skin cells to open. Because of the skin's naturally selective characteristics, items beyond the size of large molecules or bacteria are not physically able to pass through these open gates. Generally, DMSO can only deliver chemicals in aqueous solution.]<<<<<
—KAM <17:02:44/12-27-52>

OXYGENATED FLUOROCARBONS

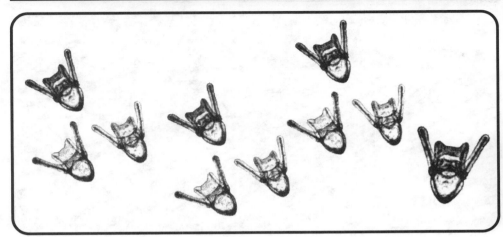

ORDER HERE

RATINGS

Legality Rating: **Legal**

Availability: **4/48 hours**

Street Index: **1**

Oxygenated fluorocarbon is a compound used as a blood substitute. Fluorocarbons are a group of organic molecules whose hydrogen atoms have been replaced with fluorine atoms. Because their structure is so different from hemoglobin, they would not appear to be likely replacements for hemoglobin as a vehicle for gaseous exchange, yet fluorocarbons actually exceed the capabilities of hemoglobin by a wide margin.

Whole blood (containing hemoglobin) dissolves 20 percent oxygen by volume; fluorocarbons dissolve 40 percent and up, plus the ability to dissolve twice as much carbon dioxide by volume than their iron-based counterpart.

Fluorocarbons were discovered as a medium for gaseous exchange in 1966, and their first practical use came in 1973; there were, however, problems. Fluorocarbons are naturally immiscible in water, and, if introduced untreated, would soon lead to death by embolism. Though researchers solved this problem by emulsifying the fluorocarbon solution as a mixture of 75 percent perflurodecalin and 25 percent perfluropropylamine, another problem was created. The emulsified fluorocarbons had a tendency to concentrate in the liver and spleen, creating the potential for damage to those organs. The half-life (time required for half a substance to dissipate or disappear) for the emulsion was 65 days, long enough for substantial fluorocarbon deposits to form.

Perfluoro-4-methyl-octahydroquinalidine (P4MO), developed in 1998, was deemed safe for use by the FDA in 2001 and had become quite common by 2009. It is stable in emulsion and, therefore, will not settle out to form deposits; P4MO is removed from the system by exhalation or perspiration without being metabolized. P4MO is used as a blood substitute (preventing type mismatch in the field and during operations) and can be introduced into a healthy subject to promote higher levels of exertion. When used in such a manner (in 5-liter treatments), P4MO adds 2 dice to all Athletics Success Tests and effectively doubles the amount of time a person may hold his breath (i.e., 90 seconds instead of 45). The benefits remain in effect as long as the level of P4MO remains constant in the individual.

The half-life of P4MO is one week. After the initial week, all benefits are lost until P4MO levels are replaced. Replacing the P4MO lost due to half-life deterioration is not recommended until fluorocarbon levels in the blood drop below 25 percent, which occurs about three weeks after initial application. If replaced too early the P4MO dramatically increases the chance of death by "bubble embolism."

Price
750¥/liter

>>>>>[Bubble embolism?!]<<<<<
—Nightfire <18:31:00/12-27-52>

>>>>>[Newly introduced P4MO attaches itself to the partly disintegrated fluorocarbon fragments left over from earlier treatments. The two molecules bond together in a way that traps a gas pocket within (much like the carcerand process). These relatively massive structures (popularly referred to as "fluorobubbles") can block the smaller blood passages and capillaries, causing an embolism.]<<<<<
—KAM <18:42:17/12-27-52>

>>>>>[Nothing funny about it, chummers. One minute you're up, the next you're fast on the way to brain death. P4MO is handy, but use it in moderation.]<<<<<
—Winger <21:29:22/12-27-52>

ORDER HERE

RATINGS

Legality Rating: **Legal**

Availability: **5/14 days**

Street Index: **7.5**

RUTHENIUM POLYMERS

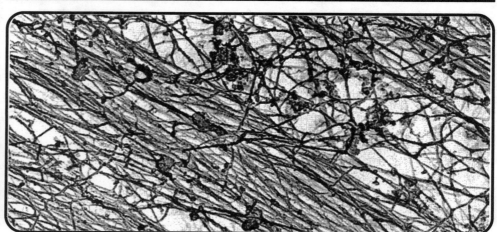

The existence of chemicals that change colors under mutable physical conditions has been known for some time. Many have, in fact, been used in modern industrial chemistry as indicators, chemical "clocks," and the basis for optical chip technology. Ruthenium polymers are exceptional cases because of their wide spectrum of colors, which can be altered easily by changing the polymer's chemical composition.

These polymers undergo color change with the application of a small voltaic charge, and they are very durable. Even after ten million color cycles, 90 percent of the material remains intact and its appearance and properties unchanged. Also, the fact that polymers can be applied in layers of less than about .1 micron thick makes it possible to apply a polymer to virtually any surface without any appreciable loss of flexibility or function. Once a current is applied, the response is almost immediate, with a delay of less than one-hundredth of a second.

Optical displays utilizing ruthenium polymers long ago replaced the outdated liquid-crystal and gas-plasma screen units and have been a key factor in increasing the portability of computing power. With the recent wedding of ruthenium-polymer technology to modern imaging technology has come about the "chameleon cloaking technology."

Chameleon technology involves scanning environmental conditions and processing the data through an imaging processor. The processed data is then fed to the ruthenium polymer surface and results in a "corrected" image of the environment—minus the cloaked object. For stealth purposes, the target numbers needed to perceive such a cloaked object are increased by +4 (e.g., a task that would normally be routine with a Target Number 4, now becomes fairly difficult at 8). At least four imaging scanners, strategically placed in order to receive full surround information, are required for the effect. More scanners give cleaner and more "correct" images. For each extra scanner beyond four, add +1 to the final target number for detection. Movement rates are not restricted because the color shifts occur fast enough to prevent image retention and optical bleeding. Radar, thermographic, and ultrasonic systems are unaffected by the effect.

Although the polymer can be applied to virtually any surface, the nature of the support electronics involved with chameleon cloaking limit the amount of armor that can be layered underneath. Any armor modified to include a ruthenium polymer surface reduces its Ballistic and Impact Rating by half (round down).

Price
10,000¥/m² + 5,000¥ for the imaging scanner

>>>>>[Ever wish you were a bandersnatch?]<<<<<
—Rapid Fire <09:04:28/12-28-52>

>>>>>[The gel packs that power the chameleon units are only good for about 30 minutes. After that you're on your own.]<<<<<
—Hatchetman <11:36:05/12-28-52>

ACTH

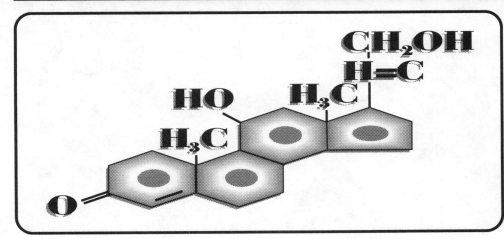

Adrenocorticotrophic hormone (ACTH), or corticotrophin, as it is more commonly known, is a naturally occurring hormone produced in the frontal lobes of the pituitary gland. Stimulating other glands of the endocrine system to produce hormones, it primarily affects the adrenal glands and causes the production of adrenalin and corticosteroids (which govern the body's use of carbohydrates).

ACTH has no real medical benefits to offer to 2052 medicine and is used primarily as a trigger for voluntary activation of the adrenal pump. Packaged in inhalers with six doses, once administered, it instantly activates the adrenal pump. Though ACTH is not addictive, a tolerance builds up over time, rendering it ineffective as an external trigger.

Addiction	Tolerance	Strength	Price
0	2	25	100¥ for 6 doses and inhaler

>>>>>[An "on" switch for your adrenal pump.]<<<<<
    —Feral <15:45:30/12-28-52>

ORDER HERE

RATINGS

Legality Rating: **Legal**

Availability: **5/12 hours**

Street Index: **1**

ATROPINE

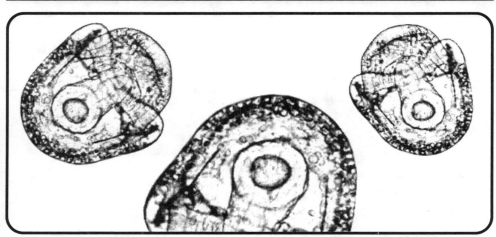

Atropine is a distilled alkaloid and the active component of the medicinal agent belladonna, which is derived from the deadly nightshade plant. Extreme in its action, it is a tranquilizer that relaxes the involuntary muscle system. Powerful and poisonous, atropine is effective in doses measuring .3 to .6 milligrams. It works internally by acting on the vagus nerve, inhibiting the actions of the organs.

Initial application results in 5D2 damage, and a +1 modifier to all Active Skill Target Numbers. The subject continues to take damage every 15 minutes until the atropine has either been neutralized or filtered out of the system. Victims of atropine poisoning experience the following symptoms: increased pulse rate, dryness of mouth, inability to focus on near objects (raising target numbers by an additional +1 for melee and close range firearms combat), mental confusion (+2 to all Knowledge, Technical, Build/Repair, Language, and Magic skills), hallucinations, hot, dry skin, and hyperpyrexia (high fever because of the inability to sweat). Some subjects may also develop a rash.

Rating	Speed	Vector	Price
5D2	Special	Injection	600¥/dose

>>>>>[Here's an interesting piece of trivia. Doctors use atropine, in extremely low concentration, to relax the muscles of the eye during eye examinations.]<<<<<
　　—The Smiling Bandit <Strikes again!/Ha-Ha-Ha>

>>>>>[Gah. Sure makes me glad I'm on good terms with my optometrist.]<<<<<
　　—Digger <21:04:31/12-28-52>

CYANIDE

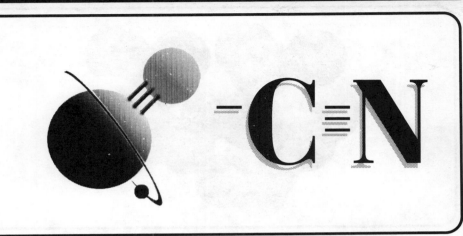

ORDER HERE

RATINGS

Legality Rating: **Legal**

Availability: **3/48 hours**

Street Index: **.5**

A salt (a compound made by replacing an acid's hydrogen, wholly or partly, with a metal) of prussic acid, cyanide is one of the most rapid-acting of all poisons. If inhaled, the effects are instantaneous; if ingested by other means, cyanide's effect occurs one minute after exposure. Its presence is noted by a momentary burning sensation in the mouth region (if the cyanide is swallowed or inhaled), the smell of bitter almonds, and an almost instant lapse into spasmodic breathing.

Cyanide works by inhibiting and blocking the action of the enzyme that controls the release of oxygen from red blood cells. The result is death by cellular asphyxiation. Oxidizing agents, such as hydrogen permanganate or potassium permanganate, can transform cyanide into a harmless oxamine, but must be applied immediately for any effect to be achieved.

Rating	Speed	Vector	Price
4D3	Immediate/1 minute	Air, ingestion, injection	360¥/dose

>>>>>[Hey, can't a guy establish and develop an immunity to a toxin by constantly exposing himself to bigger and bigger doses?]<<<<<
—The Man <23:34:47/12-28-52>

>>>>>[Yeah, sure. You can foster a complete immunity—it's called death.]<<<<<
—The Smiling Bandit <Strikes again!/Ha-Ha-Ha>

ORDER HERE

RATINGS

Legality Rating: **4-M1**

Availability: **4/24 hours**

Street Index: **.9**

HYPER

Hyper is a direct neural stimulator, acting on the nerves connected to the temporal and occipital lobes of the brain. These sections of the brain interpret most nervous sensations, including taste, smell, sound, and sight. The drug known as hyper artificially produces the effects of hyperaesthesia, a condition of excessive sensitivity to sensory stimuli, resulting in pain from even the most minor sensations. A tap, for example, feels like a sharp blow, a whisper becomes a shout, and so on.

Upon initial exposure, the victim suffers a 4S2 Stun attack and mild vertigo (apply a +1 to all target numbers). Following exposure, the victim makes a Body Success Test; each success subtracts 5 minutes from the drug's normal 60-minute effect. During this period, the individual is bombarded with intensely magnified sensations. All concentration tasks attempted in this period add +4 to their Target Numbers (including spellcasting); any damage taken (whether physical or mental) will result in additional damage because of sensory overload. This additional damage is applied to the character's Mental Condition Monitor and is calculated by halving the actual inflicted damage, rounding up. Thus, a Serious physical wound taken during the affected period would result in an additional three boxes of damage on the character's Mental Condition Monitor).

Rating	Speed	Vector	Price
4S2 Stun	Immediate	Air and injection	180¥/dose

>>>>>[This stuff is serious brain-fry. Don't get hit with hyper rounds if you can help it.]<<<<<
—The Neon Samurai <10:12:59/12-29-52>

>>>>>[It has its uses, though. Once I was on a run where our team's magical fire-support got iced early on. We'd probably have been buried when the resident mage cornered us on the grounds if Ace hadn't been packing a squirt loaded with a hyper/DMSO cocktail. A solid hit and the guy was too preoccupied to notice us buggin' out.]<<<<<
—Reflex <11:47:20/12-29-52>

KAMIKAZE

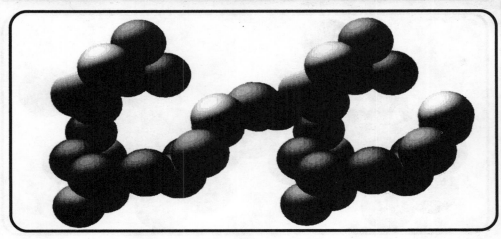

ORDER HERE

RATINGS

Legality Rating: **3-M1**

Availability: **5/4 days**

Street Index: **5**

Kamikaze is a tailored amphetamine, and is a combat drug. It has been used as a battle drug in its various forms since the 1990s, despite knowledge of its addictive and destructive nature.

In moderate doses, kamikaze can give users an edge, somewhat equalizing the odds when unaugmented (either biologically or cybernetically) individuals face augmented opponents in combat. As use continues and addiction grows, the user requires larger doses and adverse side effects begin to manifest. Large doses can cause excitement, tremors, momentary euphoria, and dilated pupils. Excess doses (bordering on overdose level) cause anxiety, hallucinations, and uncontrolled muscular movements. Even higher dosages lead quickly to death.

Used as a battle stimulant, kamikaze adds +1 Body, +1 Quickness, +2 Strength, +1 Willpower, and +1D6 to calculated Initiative. It will also negate the first four boxes of damage received (either physical or mental) after it is administered. For example, three physical boxes and one mental box, or four mental boxes, or two physical and two mental boxes, and so on. The effects of kamikaze last anywhere from 10 to 60 minutes (10 x 1D6), depending on body chemistry.

The repeated use of kamikaze has a destructive effect on the user's metabolism. On top of the regular effects of overuse, every four applications of the drug permanently subtract one box from the maximum of both the Physical and Mental Condition Monitors. After eight uses, the maximum damage an individual can withstand is eight boxes of physical and eight boxes of mental damage. This physical and mental "wasting" will eventually kill a character who intends long-term use of kamikaze. In addition, kamikaze permanently alters the bioneurological functions of the subject's body. After a number of uses equal to half the character's Body (round down), the character's bioware and cyberware will no longer function.

Despite kamikaze's many drawbacks, several institutions and companies in various parts of the world still use it as a cheap alternative to mass troop biological or cybernetic augmentation.

Attribute Bonus
+1 Body, +1 Quick, +2 Strength, +1 Willpower, +1D6 Initiative

Addiction	Tolerance	Strength	Price
4P	2	4	50¥/dose

>>>>>[Vile, disgusting stuff. We're talking really bad ju-ju here. Good thing it's illegal.]<<<<<
—Rapid Fire <12:55:43/12-29-52>

>>>>>[It is, depending on whose law you're looking at.]<<<<<
—Fastjack <13:09:14/12-29-52>

>>>>>[Well B'wana, it's mostly because of us Jokonies (read, us runners) out here that this stuff still exists. The average street-sam can walk all over a typical squad of corporate troopers. Now, the execs aren't going to spend 400,000¥ a head just to bring their grunts to our level of augmentation. Kamikaze won't make their guys a match for a good samurai, but it sure goes a long way toward evening out the odds. It's a simple matter of economics. Right now, it's a fiscally sound decision to keep using it.]<<<<<
—The Smiling Bandit <Strikes again!/Ha-Ha-Ha>

ORDER HERE

RATINGS

Legality Rating: **4-M1**

Availability: **5/36 hours**

Street Index: **2**

MAO

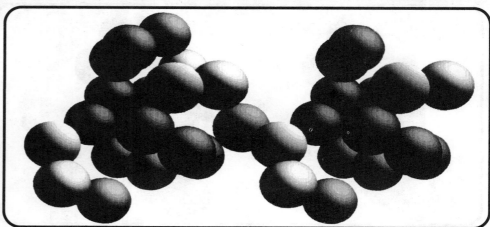

Monoamine oxidase (MAO) is an enzyme that facilitates the rapid oxidation of adrenalin, thus removing the effects of adrenalin.

Upon its injection, MAO delivers a 10L2 Stun attack. It also automatically lowers a target's Reaction Attribute by −1 and reduces the individual's Initiative by −1D6. Because MAO is a naturally occurring enzyme, there is no defense from its effects on Reaction and Initiative, although the Stun attack may be resisted normally.

On targets with an active adrenal pump, MAO further inhibits some of the pump's benefits to the character's physical attributes. An individual with a Level 1 adrenal pump receives only the Reaction bonus (his total Reaction is then modified as above). A character with a Level 2 adrenal pump receives his normal Reaction bonus (+6, but with the total Reaction modified as above), but all other attributes are modified as if he/she had only a Level 1 pump (i.e., only +1 Quickness, +1 Strength, and +1 Willpower).

MAO effects dissipate at rates dependent on situational body chemistry. To determine MAO duration, the subject makes a Body Success Test. The effects last for ten turns minus the number of resulting successes. Any further applications of MAO have no effect until the current dose has been flushed out of the subject's system.

Injectors with more controlled dosages are available to help counter the effects of the random activation of adrenal pump systems. Applications from the injector reduce the effect normally, but inflict no Stun damage. The price for injectors is 320¥ for a unit with six doses.

Rating	Speed	Vector	Price
10L2 Stun	Immediate	Injection	280¥/dose

>>>>>[Here's something else that goes a long way toward equalizing the odds for the corpers. One hit with MAO and any edge you have in speed disappears.]<<<<<
—Findler-Man <16:38:17/12-29-52>

TECHNOLOGY AND THE LAW

"Lone Star. Your friends in law enforcement; the official license-holders of the 2052 downtown Seattle contract. At Lone Star, we work hard so you can rest easy."
—Trideo ad, 2052

"Aw, skirtin' the law ain't so hard. It's like a game, see. You just gotta know how ta play."
—Debra Quinn, Collections agent, Mother's and Fathers' Ethnic Association

"Go to jail. Go directly to jail. Do not pass go. Do not collect $200."
—Game card

It is without doubt that the rapid proliferation of high-tech hardware has created a major potential for misuse of such equipment and technology. To reduce the potential for misuse and to minimize the fallout in all other situations, laws have been enacted restricting the availability and governing the control and development of sensitive technology.

Laws, and the regulated enforcement of laws, are necessary to promote a strong and stable society. Only a strong and stable society, however, can hope to maintain a fair and judicious legal system in any form. Although the legal framework for governing technological proliferation exists in many areas of the world, several governments have suffered (and some still do) from economic, political, and biological turmoil. Recovery is slow and incomplete in many communities, making it difficult to impose consistent legal restrictions on *anything*. It is not unheard of for laws and the level of enforcement to differ slightly from county to county, or even from sector to sector within the same city.

AVAILABILITY

The first way a government can place a check and balance on technological proliferation is to place restrictions on who may manufacture, sell, and possess such equipment. The **Shadowrun** rules reflect this restriction by assigning an Availability Code to each piece of equipment.

Availability is a two-part rating, representing a combination of several factors, all of them relating to how difficult it is to obtain the item. The first number in the code is an index of the item's raw availability—the higher the number, the harder it is to find the equipment.

Any time a character wishes to purchase restricted or high-tech goods, he must first locate a source and then make a Success Test against an appropriate Social Skill such as Bribery, Etiquette, Negotiation, and so on. The exact skill used depends on the situation, with the first number of the Availability Code as the Target Number. The second part of the Availability Code repre-

>>>>>[Everywhere you turn these days someone's enacting a new bill or law. Used to be if you could get something, it was legal. Drek, now you need a permit to breathe.]<<<<<
—Booster <21:55:04/12-29-52>

>>>>>[Most of this drek is just technicalities. Ultimately, the law can be boiled down to a single concept/commandment: THOU SHALT NOT GET CAUGHT.]<<<<<
—The Smiling Bandit <Strikes again!/Ha-Ha-Ha>

>>>>>[Perhaps that's the case with the law of the land, but there are higher courts and even higher powers whose reach you can't evade—at least, not forever.]<<<<<
—Fastjack <07:39:42/01-02-53>

sents the base time it takes for the character to actually get the item into his possession. If the character attempting the purchase makes a successful Social Skill Success Test, he may apply any extra successes to reduce the base time for acquisition. For instance, a character with Negotiation 4 wants to purchase an item with an Availability Code of 5/10 days. His Social Skill Test yields two successes, which indicates that his source has located the item, but will need five days to get it in stock.

Permits for possession and transport can be obtained in a similar manner for any items that require them, that is, if the individual can justify his need for such a license. A "P" in the Availability Code indicates that a permit for the object is obtainable (e.g., 4P/6 hours). To represent the inherent difficulties involved in obtaining permits for restricted equipment, add +2 to the Availability Target Number when making the necessary Success Test for purchasing permits. That is, if the item code is 4P/1 week, use a Target Number 6 to calculate permit availability and a Target Number 4 to calculate the availability of the item itself. Unless otherwise noted, the price for most permits is usually 5 percent of the sale price of the item for permission to possess, and 10 percent of the sale price for permission to possess and transport (in both cases, round up to the nearest nuyen).

Purchase of restricted items through legitimate channels usually requires the presentation of a valid license or permit. Without a permit, the only source for restricted equipment is the street or the shadow market. It is possible to obtain permits through street channels (albeit at the higher street prices).

Permits are annual and renewable (if renewal can be justified) without need for an Availability Test if the permit fee is paid before the expiration of the initial license. In many cases, government agencies, certain government licensees, and registered security and law-enforcement agencies are exempt from the need to purchase permits. They must, however, present their credentials whenever asked to do so. Items that are fully legal do not require a permit, though registered agencies may acquire licenses for equipment for which no standard license is available.

Items are generally easier to get on the street and from the gray market. When purchasing from such sources, apply the Street Index multiple, but subtract −2 from the Availability Code. Spending extra money may further reduce the difficulty of acquisition and the required waiting time. For every additional +25 percent of the purchase price (i.e., price after factoring in the Street Index) spent, reduce the Availability Target

Number by −1 (but never less than a Target Number 2) and reduce the required time by −20 percent (this reduction is made before the actual Availability Test).

Availability Tests are only made if the source is willing to carry or fence the requested item. Most fixers and street sources will shy away from items whose Availability Code is too high or that are blatantly and grossly illegal (e.g., bacterial weapons, tactical military weapons, and so on).

>>>>>[Ah yes. The court of man, and the courts of, shall we say, above. I quite agree that there are rules you simply do not break. But let's face it, that's a whole different ball game. Ninety-nine point ninety-nine percent of us here aren't even eligible to join that league, much less play or be a contender.]<<<<<
—The Smiling Bandit <Strikes again!/Ha-Ha-Ha>

>>>>>[For the last time, guys, cut out the philosophical mumbo-jumbo! I'm not tuning in for my spiritual enlightenment. SHOP TALK!]<<<<<
—Feral <10:47:18/01-02-53>

>>>>>[I never understood why so much bioware and cyberware is either under strict control or else illegal.]<<<<<
—Digger <12:01:39/01-02-53>

LEGALITY

The abrupt introduction of new technologies has spurred recent changes and ratifications to the existing legal structure relating to equipment and unlawful behavior. These changes generally expand the list of items considered restricted access and revise the list of resulting fines and jail terms.

To summarize the legal ramifications of being found guilty of possession of a restricted item, **Shadowrun** uses the Legality Rating. The Legality Rating is a two-part code. The first number represents the severity of restriction; the lower the number, the higher the level of restriction. In any casual encounter with law enforcement officials or with security personnel empowered to act as law enforcement officials, use this number as a Target Number against the officer's Security or Police Procedures Skill. (In any pursuit encounter, it is assumed that the officers will automatically consider the offenders to be dangerous unless otherwise motivated or informed.) In most cases, this test is only necessary if the attending officer either suspects the presence of restricted items or visually recognizes/identifies restricted items (the officer must make a Perception Test if the items are concealed). If the Security or Police Procedures Success Test fails, the officer does not notice any improprieties. With one success, the officer is aware of the situation, but will not make the effort to arrest the offender (although he will probably issue a warning). Any additional successes indicate that the officer will press the issue, i.e., ask the individual to present a permit (if one is available) or attempt to arrest him. Severity of restriction is flexible and very relative, fluctuating from sector to sector, depending on the level of enforcement. In low-enforcement areas, the Restriction Target Number may be increased by up to +3 (almost everyone looks the other way). Conversely, in highly enforced areas, the Target Number may drop by as much as –3 (but never less than a Target Number 2).

The second part of the Legality Rating lists the restriction category under which the object falls (see below for more details).

Generally, the Legality Rating refers to the normal Seattle/UCAS standard. Some variation in the item's legality may exist among the various multinational, extraterritorial megacorporations. What is illegal in UCAS may simply be controlled at Mitsuhama. See **Jurisdiction**, page xx, for more information.

RESTRICTED ITEMS

All restricted items are divided into categories representing similar types of items. Each category is represented by a letter code. Following is a list of categories and examples of items included in each.

Category A: Small Bladed Weapon

This includes any sharp-edged, hand-held weapon (including impromptu weapons) with a cutting edge under 18 centimeters long.

Category B: Large Bladed Weapon

This includes any sharp-edged, hand-held weapon (including impromptu weapons) with a cutting edge more than 18 centimeters long. This category also includes axes, polearms, and cybernetic blade weapons (hand razors and spurs). Permits for weapons in this category cost 100¥ for possession, 250¥ for transport.

Category C: Blunt Weapon

This includes any non-edged hand-held weapon (including impromptu weapons). This category includes clubs, batons, and all shock weapons (shock gloves and shock batons).

Category D: Projectile Weapon

This includes any weapon specifically designed for throwing, and any muscle-powered or mechanically powered ranged weapon (spears, bows, and crossbows). Permits for weapons of this category cost 125¥ for possession, 300¥ for transport.

Category E: Pistol

This includes any revolver or semi-automatic pistol, regardless of caliber. Permits for weapons of this category cost 200¥ for possession, 500¥ for transport.

Category F: Rifle

This includes any single-action rifle or manual-action shotgun (regardless of barrel length). Permits for weapons of this category cost 300¥ for possession, 600¥ for transport.

Category G: Automatic Weapon

This includes any weapon whose rate of fire exceeds one per pull (includes all assault rifles, machine pistols, and submachine guns). Special licenses are available to legitimate, registered security and law-enforcement agencies.

>>>>>[There's only one real underlying reason why anybody gets this stuff in the first place, and that's to make life difficult for somebody else. Any effort to keep the civil peace would logically include restricting who has access to such "disruptive" technology.]<<<<<
—The Smiling Bandit <Strikes again!/Ha-Ha-Ha>

>>>>>[But there's a multitude of non-lethal, non-aggressive applications for bioware and cyberware.]<<<<<
—Digger <17:24:56/01-02-53>

>>>>>[Laws are drafted to deal with the "worst" elements of human nature. Where both beneficial and destructive factors are present, more often than not it is the destructive side that is primarily considered.]<<<<<
—Fastjack <19:11:20/01-02-53>

Category H: Heavy Weapon

This includes all cannons, machine guns, and other heavy-caliber weapons. Special licenses are available to legitimate, registered security and law-enforcement agencies.

Category I: Explosives

This includes all explosives, including propelled (HE rounds) or demolition charges. Special licenses are available to legitimate, registered security and law-enforcement agencies.

Category J: Military Weapon

This includes any military-grade/issued weapon not specifically covered by other categories. Special licenses are available to legitimate, registered security and law-enforcement agencies.

Category K: Military Armor

This includes any armor (whether partial or full) intended for law enforcement, military, or security work. Special licenses are available to legitimate, registered security and law-enforcement agencies.

Category L: Military Ammunition

This includes any special-purpose ammunition (APDS, FL, and such) designated for law enforcement, military, or security use. Special licenses are available to legitimate, registered security and law-enforcement agencies.

Class A Bioware (BA)

This includes all bioware of a paralegal nature, including damage compensators, orthoskin, pain editors, and trauma dampers. Permits are available (only possession required).

Class B Bioware (BB)

This includes all bioware designated for law enforcement, military, or security work. This includes adrenal pump, muscle augmentation, suprathyroids, synaptic accelerators, and toxin exhalers. Permits are available (only possession required, but cost is 10 percent of sale price).

Class C Bioware (BC)

This includes all military-grade bioware, including adrenal pump-2, muscle augmentation-3 (and higher), and synaptic accelerator-2. Special licenses are available to legitimate, registered security and law-enforcement agencies.

Category CA: Class A Cyberware

This includes all cyberware of a paralegal nature. This includes bone lacing (plastic), crypto circuit HD, dermal plating, internal voice masks, smartgun links, and vehicle control rigs. Permits are available (only possession required).

Category CB: Class B Cyberware

This includes all cyberware designated for law enforcement, military, or security work. This includes bone lacing (aluminum), boosted reflexes, muscle replacement, program carrier, scramble breaker HD, Level 1 tactical computer, and wired reflexes. Permits are available (only possession required, but cost is 10 percent of sale price).

Category CC: Class C Cyberware

This covers all military-grade cyberware, including bone lacing (titanium), cortex bombs, cranial cyberdecks, cyberweapons, Level 3 muscle replacement (and higher), Level 2 tactical computer (and higher), and Level 3 wired reflexes. Special licenses are available to legitimate, registered security and law-enforcement agencies.

Category CD: Class D Matrix Technology

This includes all unregistered cyberdecks and Matrix program software. Special licenses are available to legitimate, registered security and law-enforcement agencies.

Category E1: Class A Equipment

This includes all equipment of a paralegal nature, including jammers and laser microphones. Permits are available (only possession required).

Category E2: Class B Equipment

This covers all equipment designated for law enforcement, military, or security work, including data codebreakers, dataline taps, maglock passkeys, and voice identifiers. Permits are available (only possession required, but cost is 10 percent of sale price).

Category E3: Class C Equipment

This includes all military-grade equipment. Special licenses are available to legitimate, registered security and law-enforcement agencies.

Category M1: Class A Controlled

This includes controlled chemicals and pharmaceuticals.

Category M2: Class B Controlled

This includes controlled neural electronics (BTLs and hypersim).

Category M3: Class C Controlled

This includes microbiological-warfare agents.

>>>>>[I don't think that giving corporations any measure of legal power was a wise decision on the government's part.]<<<<<
—Rapid Fire <20:32:41/01-02-53>

>>>>>[What makes you think that anybody in government had any choice? These are companies that make significantly more nuyen then several countries. That makes for a lot of lobbying power.]<<<<<
—Fastjack <22:47:03/01-02-53>

>>>>>[Some of these companies maintain a surprisingly good enforcement team, and have quite an extended reach. Point of fact: don't mess with the phone company. The entire telephone net is considered one gigantic "installation" as far as jurisdiction is concerned. Wherever there's phone service, the phone cops can nail you. Since almost all illegal use of the Matrix is done through

CRIMINAL OFFENSES

Weapons and equipment-related offenses vary from simple possession to use with intent. These offenses carry a number rating. When an individual is charged with a weapons/equipment offense, the code used to designate the offense is the weapon classification followed by the weapon offense number. For example, use of an assault rifle would be a G4 offense. Weapon/equipment offenses are listed below.

Possession (1)

The owning or carrying of equipment or weapons designated as restricted access.

Transport (2)

The act of carrying or transporting said items, either on one's person or in a vehicle.

Threat (3)

The act of brandishing a weapon in public, regardless of whether the weapon is used intentionally to threaten (carrying an externally visible weapon, such as a gun stuck through a belt, is considered a threat).

Use (4)

Use of any weapon against living targets, public or private property, and any usage in the general vicinity of living targets, public or private property. This offense is concerned only with actual usage, not any harm (or intent to harm) resulting from the weapon's use.

Intent (5)

Use of any weapon against living targets, public or private property, and any usage in the general vicinity of living targets, public or private property intended explicitly to cause physical injury or property damage (regardless of whether injury or damage actually occurred).

CRIMINAL CHARGES

Weapon and equipment-related offenses are rarely filed alone. They are usually submitted along with other, more serious criminal charges. This is not to say, however, that they are never filed independently. Law enforcement officers will not hesitate to take the time to charge an individual armed with an assault cannon.

Following is a list of some of the various criminal charges. Other charges do exist, but these are the most common.

Arson

The intentional setting on fire of a building or property.

Assault

Any threat to cause physical harm or an unsuccessful attempt to do so.

Battery

Any illegal beating or touching of another person, either directly or with an object.

Extortion

The use of threats or violence to acquire goods, money, or services.

Forcible Confinement

The imprisonment or restraint of an individual against his will.

Fraud

Any use of intentional deception to cause a person to give up property or some legal right.

Illegal Entry

Any intrusion into property, without rightful access, whether overt or clandestine (includes the lesser charge of trespassing).

Kidnapping

Using force or fraud to seize and hold or carry off an individual against his will.

Larceny

Theft: the unlawful taking away of another's property without consent, and with the intention of depriving him of it. Larceny may be broken down into two categories: petty (1,000¥ or less), and grand (more than 1,000¥).

Murder 1

First-degree murder. A charge of premeditated murder is difficult to prove, and is thus rarely filed. To be charged with Murder 1, it must be proved that the suspect planned and conspired to kill his victim.

Murder 2

Homicide. Second-degree murder is the charge filed when direct intent to kill is provable, but when it is not possible to prove premeditation. For example, if a bar patron suddenly gets angry, pulls out a gun and shoots the man sitting next to him, the charge is homicide. Intent to kill is obvious, but there is no indication of premeditation.

phone lines and LTG access, the phone company has a vested interest in going after deckers. If you're logged in, you're definitely in their jurisdiction. Watch out, chummers, you never know when Ma Bell and her boys are watching.]<<<<<
—The Smiling Bandit <Strikes again!/Ha-Ha-Ha>

>>>>>[Actually, Mr. Bandit, your bringing up Matrix access reminds me of something I've been meaning to ask you for a long time. How do you alter those time/date stamps? According to my understanding of network mechanics and technology, the time/date stamp is appended to net activity by hardware and software inherent in the LTG system itself. It's there so that the phone company can (theoretically) track access and use. I suppose the system could be overridden, but that would only yield a null stamp, not a definable segment of text like you have. Doing so would also trip the tampering alarms.]<<<<<
—KAM <08:44:07/01-03-53>

Murder 3

Manslaughter. Any action that results in the accidental death of an individual. In cases where death occurs but the intent to kill is not provable, the charge usually drops to manslaughter.

Negligence

Negligence is the failure to exercise a reasonable amount of care, resulting in the injury or death of another.

Rape

Any forced act of sexual intercourse. Statutory rape involves violation of a minor.

Reckless Endangerment

Any action, deliberate or accidental, where injury or death is averted only by sheer luck.

Solicitation

The act of tempting or enticing another individual into wrongdoing.

Trafficking

The buying or selling of illegal or restricted goods.

Treason

Any act that results in the betrayal of allegiance, including the levying of war, adhering to the enemy, and providing the enemy with aid and "comfort."

Vandalism

The malicious or ignorant, willful destruction of property.

REDUCED CHARGES

In some cases, the criminal charge may be tempered by events or plea-bargaining, in which case the charge may be altered by the following conditions.

Accessory

The accessory charge applies in any case where the individual may not be directly involved in the commission of a crime, but may have given aid to the perpetrators.

Conspiracy

Conspiracy involves individuals acting or planning together for an unlawful purpose (e.g., conspiracy to commit fraud, conspiracy to commit murder, and so on).

JURISDICTION

The boundaries that separate the legal jurisdiction of various prosecuting bodies has blurred somewhat since their initial establishment more than 275 years ago. Crimes today generally fall under three classifications: federal, corporate, and local.

Federal law enforcement agencies tend to hold the greatest power and are the most free to exercise that power. In most countries federal jurisdiction covers: computer crime, congressional laws, controlled or restricted-access equipment and materials, corporate crime, crimes committed in federally controlled areas, crimes crossing state lines, crimes involving foreign nationals, crimes involving government offices, kidnapping, terrorism, and treason.

When the multinational megacorporations were granted partial extraterritorial status in 2001, several laws were altered to give these new "micro-nations" a measure of semi-independence. The megacorporations do not have the same spectrum of power that federal agencies enjoy, but their legal reach does stretch beyond national borders. Corporate jurisdiction covers crimes involving the corporate body and crimes involving corporate assets or employees. Punishment for violation of corporate laws is wholly the responsibility of the "governing" corporate board of directors, and thus varies from company to company.

Jurisdiction on the local level is the most vague. For instance, although a local law enforcement department may have a vice squad, the enforcement of controlled substances technically falls under federal jurisdiction. Basically, local law enforcement handles most minor criminal infractions and attempts to keep the peace. Major crimes involving large-scale operations and restricted-access equipment are usually tackled in cooperation with federal authorities or simply handed over to

>>>>>[Oh, sure. I tell you. You tell somebody else. Next thing I know, everybody'll be doing it. The phone company won't be able to track anybody's access. You know what, doc? You may actually be onto something here.]<<<<<
—The Smiling Bandit <Strikes again!/Ha-Ha-Ha>

the federal agencies outright. Cities with understaffed police forces usually subcontract out to licensed security companies for essential services. In such cases, employees of the security companies are considered deputized officers of the law for the term of the contract.

Several problems exist within the current three-tiered system of legal jurisdiction, the most obvious being the partial extraterritorial status of megacorporations. Within the actual grounds of a corporation's compound, the laws of the megacorporation are paramount, as long as no crime is committed on or against a federal body. For example, within the Ares Weapons complex it would be no offense to carry a military weapon, even though UCAS considers such possession a crime. Possession is completely legal under Ares' employee/position-based legal code as long as the weapon is not used to commit a crime against a federal body or representative, e.g., shooting an FBI agent.

Although this distinction in jurisdiction is relatively straightforward within the corporate complex, jurisdiction becomes a dicey situation outside those bounds. That is why the results of confrontation with law enforcement officials will vary within the same sector, depending on whose law enforcement department is encountered. For example, the above Ares "citizen," if stopped by a member of Knight Errant, the Ares enforcement arm, would just be motioned on his way. A UCAS officer or even a Seattle officer, on the other hand, would have him behind bars as soon as possible. Then again, the reverse might occur if the law enforcement official were from Lone Star. This jurisdictional overlap becomes even more complicated when several companies have major operations within the same area (as happens in most metropolitan centers). Generally, the federal authorities exercise the greatest amount of influence in these "buffer zones," with local authorities coming a close second. (In many instances local authorities are the corporate authorities, especially in dormitory communities.) However, it is not unknown for megacorporations to press for release of their "citizens" or to file for extradition/deportation if it is to their benefit.

SENTENCING AND PUNISHMENT

Sentencing and punishment vary on the local and federal levels (corporate justice is usually sentenced according to local jurisprudence).

Federal agencies will generally prosecute weapon, injury, and death offenses only if the crime occurred in connection with another crime falling under federal jurisdiction. Even so, weapons offenses for possession and transport are almost never pursued on a federal level.

The following list of fines and imprisonment terms are the typical judicial call. Mitigating circumstances may reduce or increase sentences (e.g., first-time offense versus repeat offender), as might plea-bargaining.

Unless otherwise noted, most sentences include the potential for parole after the offender has served at least 30 percent of the prison term. If parole is granted, the individual must remain on parole for at least another 20 percent of his total sentence.

LOCAL FINES AND PUNISHMENT (SEATTLE)

Category	1 Possession	2 Transport	3 Threat	4 Use	5 Intent
(A) Small Blade	100¥	500¥	1,000¥	2,000¥/2 mths	5,000¥/6 mths
(B) Large Blade	200¥	800¥	2,000¥	5,000¥/4 mths	10,000¥/8 mths
(C) Blunt Weapon	150¥	650¥	1,500¥	3,000¥/3 mths	7,000¥/8 mths
(D) Projectile	300¥	1,000¥	2,000¥	3,000¥/4 mths	5,000¥/8 mths
(E) Pistol	500¥	1,500¥	5,000¥	10,000¥/1 yr	10,000¥/2 yrs
(F) Rifle	1,000¥	3,000¥	8,000¥	8,000¥/18 mths	8,000¥/3 yrs
(G) Automatic Weapon	5,000¥	10,000¥	10,000¥/6 mths	10,000¥/2 yrs	10,000¥/4 yrs
(H) Heavy Weapon	10,000¥	20,000¥	20,000¥/1 yr	20,000¥/4 yrs	20,000¥/10 yrs
(I) Explosives	10,000¥	40,000¥	40,000¥/1 yr	40,000¥/4 yrs	40,000¥/10 yrs
(J) Military Weapon	10,000¥/6 mths	10,000¥/1 yr	10,000¥/2 yrs	10,000¥/8 yrs	10,000¥/20 yrs
(K) Military Armor	1,200¥				
(L) Military Ammunition	3,000¥				
(BA) Class A Bioware	4,000¥				
(BB) Class B Bioware	12,000¥				
(BC) Class C Bioware	12,000¥/3 yrs				
(CA) Class A Cyberware	5,000¥/3 yrs				
(CB) Class B Cyberware	15,000¥				
(CC) Class C Cyberware	15,000¥/3 yrs				
(CD) Class D Matrix Tech	8,000¥/2 yrs				
(EA) Class A Equipment	2,000¥				
(EB) Class B Equipment	4,000¥				
(EC) Class C Equipment	8,000¥/2 yrs				
(MA) Class A Controlled	500¥/1 mth				
(MB) Class B Controlled	2,000¥/1 mth				
(MC) Class C Controlled	federal				

FEDERAL FINES AND PUNISHMENT (UCAS)

Category	1 Possession	2 Transport	3 Threat	4 Use	5 Intent
(A) Small Blade			2,500¥/3 mths	5,000¥/6 mths	10,000¥/1 yr
(B) Large Blade			2,500¥/3 mths	5,000¥/6 mths	10,000¥/1 yr
(C) Blunt Weapon			2,500¥/3 mths	5,000¥/6 mths	10,000¥/1 yr
(D) Projectile			2,500¥/3 mths	5,000¥/6 mths	10,000¥/1 yr
(E) Pistol			5,000¥/1 yr	10,000¥/2 yrs	25,000¥/3 yrs
(F) Rifle			5,000¥/1 yr	10,000¥/2 yrs	25,000¥/3 yrs
(G) Automatic Weapon	5,000¥	10,000¥/3 mths	25,000¥/2 yrs	25,000¥/4 yrs	50,000¥/5 yrs
(H) Heavy Weapon	10,000¥/2 yrs	20,000¥/2 yrs	30,000¥/5 yrs	30,000¥/7 yrs	30,000¥/10 yrs
(I) Explosives	500¥	2,500¥/3 mths	2,500¥/3 yrs	2,500¥/10 yrs	2,500¥/15 yrs
(J) Military Weapon	10,000¥/2 yrs	20,000¥/2 yrs	20,000¥/5 yrs	20,000¥/7 yrs	20,000¥/10 yrs
(K) Military Armor	5,000¥				
(L) Military Ammunition	1,000¥				
(BA) Class A Bioware	4,000¥				
(BB) Class B Bioware	8,000¥				
(BC) Class C Bioware	12,000¥/3 yrs				
(CA) Class A Cyberware	5,000¥				
(CB) Class B Cyberware	10,000¥				
(CC) Class C Cyberware	15,000¥/6 mths				
(CD) Class D Matrix Tech	6,000¥/6 mths				
(EA) Class A Equipment	1,500¥				
(EB) Class B Equipment	3,000¥/3 mths				
(EC) Class C Equipment	6,000¥/6 mths				
(MA) Class A Controlled	500¥				
(MB) Class B Controlled	1,000¥				
(MC) Class C Controlled	25,000¥/10 yrs				

CRIMINAL CHARGES

Type	Sentence
Arson	5,000¥/1 yr
Assault	2,000¥/1 yr
Battery	2,500¥/1 yr
Extortion	2–3 yrs
Forcible Confinement	2–5 yrs
Fraud	2–5 yrs
Illegal Entry	1–5 yrs
Kidnapping	5–10 yrs
Larceny (petty)	2–5 yrs
Larceny (grand)	2–10 yrs
Murder 1	30 yrs–life (no parole)*
Murder 2	10 yrs–life
Murder 3	2–5 yrs
Negligence	1–5 yrs
Rape	2–5 yrs
Rape (statutory)	2–10 yrs
Reckless Endangerment	5,000¥/100 yrs
Solicitation	2,000¥
Trafficking	25,000¥/2–5 yrs
Treason	10 yrs–life
Vandalism	2,000¥
Accessory	20 percent normal
Conspiracy	50 percent normal

*Some jurisdictions maintain the Death Penalty for Murder One. Seattle does not.

EQUIPMENT TABLE

This table is a complete list of all personal equipment described in this book and previous **Shadowrun** products. A Legality Rating, Availability Code, and Street Index have now been assigned to each of these items.

WEAPONS

	Type	Concealability	Base Price	Legality	Availability	Street Index
PISTOLS						
Streetline Special	Hold-out	8	100¥	10P-E	2/12 hrs	.75
Tiffani Self-Defender	Hold-out	8	450¥	10P-E	2/12 hrs	.75
Walther Palm Pistol	Hold-out	9	200¥	10P-E	3/12 hrs	.75
Ares Light Fire 70	Light	5	475¥	8P-E	3/12 hrs	.8
Beretta 200ST	Light	4	750¥	6-G	5/24 hrs	1.5
Beretta Model 101T	Light	5	350¥	8P-E	3/12 hrs	.8
Ceska vz/120	Light	7	500¥	8P-E	3/12 hrs	.8
Colt America L36	Light	6	350¥	8P-E	3/12 hrs	.8
Fichetti Security 500	Light	7	400¥	8P-E	3/12 hrs	.8
Fichetti Security 500a	Light	6	450¥	8P-E	3/12 hrs	.8
Seco LD-120	Light	5	400¥	8P-E	3/12 hrs	.8
Ares Crusader MP	Light (MP)	6	950¥	5-G	5/36 hrs	2
Ceska Black Scorpion	Light (MP)	6	750¥	5-G	5/36 hrs	2
Ares Predator	Heavy	5	450¥	6P-E	3/24 hrs	.5
Ares Predator II	Heavy	4	550¥	6P-E	4/24 hrs	1.25
Ares Viper Slivergun	Heavy	6	600¥	6P-E	3/48 hrs	1
Browning Max-Power	Heavy	6	450¥	6P-E	3/24 hrs	1
Browning Ultra-Power	Heavy	6	525¥	6P-E	4/24 hrs	1.5
Colt Manhunter	Heavy	5	425¥	6P-E	4/24 hrs	1
Remington Roomsweeper	Heavy	8	500¥	6P-E	3/24 hrs	1
Ruger Super Warhawk	Heavy	4	300¥	6P-E	3/24 hrs	1
SPECIAL WEAPONS						
Ares Squirt	Light	7	750¥	4-E	8/3 days	2
Narcoject Pistol	Light	7	600¥	4P-E	6/2 days	2
Narcoject Rifle	Shotgun	4	1,700¥	4P-F	8/2 days	2
Defiance Super Shock	"Light"	4	1,000¥	6P-E	5/24 hrs	1
Normal Net Gun	"SMG"	4	750¥	6P-E	8/36 hrs	2
Large Net Gun	"SMG"	3	1,150¥	6P-E	8/36 hrs	2
SUBMACHINE GUNS						
AK-97 SMG/Carbine	SMG	4	800¥	4-G	5/3 days	1
Beretta Model 70	SMG	3	900¥	4-G	5/3 days	1
Heckler & Koch HK227	SMG	4	1,500¥	4-G	4/24 hrs	.75
HK227-S	SMG	5	1,200¥	3-G	10/7 days	2
Heckler & Koch MP-5TX	SMG	5	850¥	4-G	5/36 hrs	1
Ingram Smartgun	SMG	5	950¥	4-G	4/24 hrs	1
Sandler TMP	SMG	4	500¥	4-G	5/36 hrs	1
SCK Model 100 SMG	SMG	4	1,000¥	4-G	5/36 hrs	1
Steyr AUG-CSL	SMG	5	*See note	3G	10/4 days	3
Uzi III	SMG	5	600¥	4-G	4/24 hrs	.75

	Type	Concealability	Base Price	Legality	Availability	Street Index
RIFLES						
Remington 750	Sporting	3	600¥	5P-F	3/24 hrs	1
Remington 950	Sporting	2	800¥	5P-F	3/24 hrs	1
Ruger 100	Sporting	2	1,300¥	5P-F	3/24 hrs	1
Steyr AUG-CSL Carbine	Sporting	3	*See note	3-F	10/4 days	3
Ranger Arms SM-3	Sniper	—	4,000¥	2-J	12/7 days	4
Walther WA 2100	Sniper	—	6,500¥	2-J	12/7 days	4
Enfield AS-7	Shotgun	3	1,000¥	5P-F	3/24 hrs	1
Defiance T-250	Shotgun	4	500¥	5P-F	3/24 hrs	1
Mossberg CMDT	Shotgun	2	1,400¥	5-F	4/48 hrs	1
Mossberg CMDT/SM	Shotgun	2	1,900¥	3-F	8/4 days	2
AK-97	Assault	3	700¥	2-G	3/36 hrs	2
AK-98	Assault/GR	—	2,500¥	1-G	8/4 days	4
Colt M22a2	Assault	3	1,600¥	2-G	4/3 days	2
FN HAR	Assault	2	1,200¥	2-G	4/48 hrs	2
H&K G12A3z	Assault	2	2,200¥	2-G	8/4 days	3
Samopal vz 88V	Assault	2	1,800¥	2-G	5/36 hrs	2
Steyr AUG-CSL AR	Assault	2	*See note	2-G	10/4 days	3
GRENADE LAUNCHER						
Generic Under-Barrel	GR	–3	1,700¥	1-JI	8/4 days	3
LIGHT MACHINE GUNS						
Ares MP-LMG	Light	—	2,200¥	2-H	6/5 days	2
GE Vindicator Minigun	Light	—	12,500¥	1-J	24/14 days	2
Ingram Valiant	Light	—	1,500¥	1-H	6/5 days	2
Steyr AUG CSL	Light	—	*See note	2-H	10/4 days	3

*The entire Steyr AUG-CSL package with all listed accessories costs 4,500¥. The weapon also comes with Gas-Vent 1 recoil reduction.

	Type	Concealability	Base Price	Legality	Availability	Street Index
LASER WEAPONS						
Ares MP Laser	"Sniper"	—	2.5 million ¥	1-J	NA	NA
HEAVY WEAPONS						
FN MAG-5 MMG	MMG	—	3,200¥	2-H	18/14 days	3
Generic MMG	MMG	—	2,500¥	2-H	14/14 days	2
Generic HMG	HMG	—	4,000¥	2-H	18/14 days	2
Stoner-Ares M107	HMG	—	5,200¥	2-H	18/14 days	3
Assault Cannon	Cannon	—	6,500¥	2-H	16/14 days	2
Panther Assault Cannon	Cannon	—	7,200¥	2-H	16/14 days	2
MISSILE LAUNCHERS						
High-Explosive (HEM)	Missile	—	1,500¥	1-K	12/14 days	3
Anti-Personnel (APM)	Missile	—	1,000¥	1-K	12/14 days	3
Anti-Vehicle (AVM)	Missile	—	2,000¥	1-K	12/14 days	3
Surface-to-Air (SAM)	Missile	—	2,200¥	1-K	18/21 days	4
Multi-Launcher (4-break)	—	—	8,000¥	1-K	12/14 days	2

	Concealability	Base Price	Legality	Availability	Street Index
MELEE WEAPONS					
Edged Weapons					
Ares Monosword	3	2,500¥	4-B	4/24 hrs	1
Centurion Laser Axe	2	3,500¥	4-B	3/24 hrs	.5
Combat Axe	2	750¥	3-B	3/24 hrs	2
Katana	3	1,000¥	5-B	4/48 hrs	2
Knife	8	30¥	8-A	2/4 hrs	.75
Survival Knife	6	450¥	6-A	3/6 hrs	1
Sword	4	500¥	4-B	3/24 hrs	1
Pole Arms/Staffs					
Pole Arm	2	500¥	3-B	4/48 hrs	2
Staff	2	50¥	8-C	3/24 hrs	1
Clubs					
Club	5	10¥	6-C	2/6 hrs	1
AZ-150 Stun Baton	5	1,500¥	5-C	3/36 hrs	2
Sap	8	10¥	5-C	2/6 hrs	1
Stun Baton	4	750¥	5-C	3/36 hrs	1
Other					
Forearm Snap Blades	7	850¥	4-B	4/48 hrs	2
Hand Razors, Extended	NA	4,500	3-B	3/72 hrs	1
Hand Razors, Retractable	10	9,000¥	3-B	3/72 hrs	1
Improved Blade	As razor	+8,500¥	3-B	6/72 hrs	1
Shock Glove	9	950¥	5-B	5/48 hrs	2
Spurs	NA	7,000¥	3-B	3/72 hrs	1
Spurs, Retractable	9	11,500¥	3-B	3/72 hrs	1
Whips/Flails					
Monofilament Whip	10	3,000¥	1-J	24/14 days	3
PROJECTILE WEAPONS					
Bows					
Bow	3	300¥	5-D	3/36 hrs	1
Arrows	3	10¥	10-D	3/36 hrs	1
Ranger–X Compound Bow	4	550¥	5-D	4/36 hrs	2
Ranger–X Precision Arrows	3	18¥	10-D	4/36 hrs	2
Crossbows					
Light	2	300¥	6-D	4/36 hrs	1
Medium	2	400¥	6-D	5/36 hrs	1
Heavy	NA	500¥	5-D	6/36 hrs	1
Bolts	4	5¥	10-D	5/36 hrs	1
THROWING WEAPONS					
Non-Aerodynamic					
Throwing Knife	9	20¥	8-D	2/24 hrs	1
Aerodynamic					
Shuriken	8	30¥	6-D	2/24 hrs	2

	Concealability	Base Price	Legality	Availability	Street Index
CLOTHING AND ARMOR					
Armor Clothing	10	500¥	Legal	2/36 hrs	1
Armor Jacket	7	900¥	Legal	3/36 hrs	.75
Armor Vest	12	200¥	Legal	2/36 hrs	.8
Vest With Plates	10	600¥	Legal	3/36 hrs	1
Secure Clothing	12	450¥	Legal	3/36 hrs	.9
Secure Jacket	9	850¥	Legal	4/36 hrs	.8
Secure Vest	15	175¥	Legal	3/36 hrs	.9
Secure Ultra-Vest	14	350¥	Legal	4/36 hrs	.9
Secure Long Coat	10	650¥	Legal	3/36 hrs	.9
Lined Coat	8	700¥	Legal	2/24 hrs	.75
Form-Fitting Body Armor					
Level 1	—	150¥	Legal	3/48 hrs	1
Level 2	15	250¥	Legal	4/48 hrs	1
Level 3	12	500¥	Legal	4/48 hrs	1
Forearm Guards	12	250¥	Legal	5/36 hrs	.75
Heavy Armor					
Partial Suit	—	10,000¥	4P-K	8/10 days	2
Full Suit	—	20,000¥	2P-K	16/14 days	3
Light Security	—	7,500¥	4P-K	12/10 days	2
Medium Security	—	9,000¥	3P-K	14/10 days	2.5
Heavy Security	—	12,000¥	2P-K	16/14 days	3
Security Helmet	—	250¥	(−1)P-K	12/14 days	2
Helmet	—	200¥	(−1)P-K	12/14 days	1.5
Small Riot Shield	—	1,500¥	Legal	8/14 days	2
Large Riot Shield	—	3,200¥	Legal	8/14 days	2
Leather					
Real	—	750¥	Legal	Always	.75
Synthetic	—	250¥	Legal	Always	.6
AMMUNITION, per 10 shots					
Regular Ammo	8	20¥	As weapon	2/24 hrs	.75
Explosive Round	8	50¥	As weapon	3/36 hrs	.8
Flechette Round	8	100¥	As weapon	3/36 hrs	.8
Firepower™ Round	8	35¥	As weapon	3/36 hrs	.75
APDS Rounds	8	70¥	3-L	14/14 days	4
Gel Round	8	30¥	As weapon	4/48 hrs	1
Stun Round	6	100¥	As weapon	4/48 hrs	1
Assault Cannon Ammo	3	450¥	As weapon	5/3 days	2
Belt 100	Yeah, right	4,250¥	As weapon	8/3 days	2
Taser Dart	3	50¥	As weapon	6/36 hrs	1.5
Taser Cartridge	4	100¥	As weapon	6/36 hrs	1.5
Narcoject Rounds	8	200¥	As weapon	As weapon	As weapon

• −1 Concealability per extra 10 rounds normal ammo

•• Belted Ammo: Add rounds/100 to Availability, subtract same from first Legality number.

	Concealability	Base Price	Legality	Availability	Street Index
FIREARM and WEAPON ACCESSORIES					
Concealable Holster	+2 to weapon	100¥	Legal	2/24 hrs	.75
Grenade Launcher	–3	1,700¥	2-J	8/5 days	3
Laser Sights	–1	500¥	Legal	6/36 hrs	.9
Rangefinder	—	150¥	Legal	2/24 hrs	.8
Grenade Link	—	750¥	6-J	8/48 hrs	2
Ultrasound Sight	–2	1,300¥	Legal	8/4 days	.8
Imaging Scopes					
Low-Light	–2	1,500¥	Legal	3/36 hrs	.8
Thermographic	–2	1,500¥	Legal	3/36 hrs	.8
Magnification 1	–1	500¥	Legal	3/36 hrs	.8
Magnification 2	–1	800¥	Legal	3/36 hrs	.9
Magnification 3	–1	1,200¥	Legal	3/36 hrs	1
Recoil Compensators and Gyros					
Shock Pads	—	200¥	Legal	2/24 hrs	.75
GasVent 2	–1	450¥	Legal	2/24 hrs	.8
Improved Gas Vent 2	—	550¥	Legal	2/24 hrs	.9
Gas Vent 3	–2	700¥	Legal	2/24 hrs	1
Improved Gas Vent 3	–1	800¥	Legal	2/24 hrs	.9
Improved Gas Vent 4	–2	1,000¥	Legal	2/24 hrs	1
Gyro Mount	–5	2,500¥	Legal	4/48 hrs	1
Improved Gyro Mount	–6	3,500¥	Legal	6/48 hrs	1
Deluxe Gyro Mount	–6	6,000¥	Legal	4/48 hrs	1
Improved Deluxe Gyro Mount	–7	7,800¥	Legal	6/48 hrs	1
Other Accessories					
Bow Accessory Mount	–1	100¥	Legal	2/24 hrs	.9
Spare Clips/Magazines	—	12¥	Legal	2/24 hrs	.75
Improved Clips/Magazines	—	See SSC*	Legal	2/24 hrs	.75
Silencer	–1	500¥	As weapon	4/48 hrs	2
Smart Goggles	—	3,000¥	4P-CA	3/36 hrs	1
Smartgun Adapter	–2	1.5 x Gun Cost	4P-CA	4/48 hrs	1
Smartgun Variant	—	2 x Gun Cost	—	+1/as listed	+.5 to weapon
Ultrasound Goggles	—	1,100¥	Legal	3/36 hrs	1

*See p. 34, Street Samurai Catalog

EXPLOSIVES

Grenades	Concealability	Base Price	Legality	Availability	Street Index
Offensive	6	30¥	3-I	4/4 days	2
IPE Offensive	6	50¥	3-I	5/4 days	2
Defensive	6	30¥	3-I	4/4 days	2
IPE Defensive	6	50¥	3-I	5/4 days	2
Concussion	6	30¥	3-I	5/4 days	2
IPE Concussion	6	50¥	3-I	5/4 days	2
Gas (Neuro-Stun VII)	5	60¥	3-I	8/4 days	2
Mini-grenade	8	50¥	2-I	8/4 days	2
IPE Mini-grenade	8	80¥	2-I	8/4 days	2
Air-timed Mini-grenade	8	150¥	2-1	10/4 days	2
Smoke	5	40¥	Legal	3/36 hrs	1
Flash Grenade	6	40¥	2-I	4/48 hrs	1
Flash-Pak	12	250¥	Legal	3/36 hrs	1
Explosives, Per Kilo					
Commercial	6	60¥	4P-I	6/48 hrs	1
Plastic, Compound 4	6	80¥	4-I	8/48 hrs	1
Plastic, Compound 12	6	200¥	3-I	10/48 hrs	2
Accessories					
Timer	6	100¥	6-I	4/48 hrs	2
Radio Detonator	8	250¥	6-I	4/48 hrs	2

CYBERTECH

HEADWARE	Essence Cost	Price	Legality	Availability	Street Index
Communications					
Chipjack	.2	1,000¥	Legal	3/72 hrs	.9
Softlink (Level 1)	.15	1,000Y	Legal	3/72 hrs	.9
Level 2	.2	2,000¥	Legal	3/72 hrs	.9
Level 3	.25	4,000¥	Legal	3/72 hrs	.9
Level 4	.3	8,000¥	Legal	3/72 hrs	.9
Datajack (**SR** rules)	.2	1,000¥	Legal	Always	.9
Datajack					
Level 1	.1	500¥	Legal	Always	.9
Level 2	.15	1,000¥	Legal	Always	.9
Level 3	.2	2,000¥	Legal	Always	.9
Level 4	.25	4,000¥	Legal	Always	.9
Commlink II	.3	8,000¥	Legal	2/48 hrs	1
Commlink IV	.3	18,000¥	Legal	3/48 hrs	1.25
Commlink VIII	.3	40,000¥	Legal	4/48 hrs	1.5
Commlink X	.3	60,000¥	Legal	5/48 hrs	1.75
Crypto Circuit HD					
Level 1–4	.1	Level x 10,000¥	4P-CA	6/36 hrs	1
Level 5–7	.1	Level x 20,000¥	4P-CA	6/36 hrs	1.25
Level 8–9	.1	Level x 30,000¥	3P-CA	8/36 hrs	1.5
Level 10	.1	Level x 50,000¥	3P-CA	9/36 hrs	2
Scramble Breaker HD					
Level 1–4	.2	Level x 20,000¥	3-CB	6/48 hrs	1.5
Level 5–7	.2	Level x 40,000¥	3-CB	8/48 hrs	1.75
Level 8	.2	600,000¥	3-CB	10/48 hrs	1.75
Radio	.75	4,000¥	Legal	2/24 hrs	.8
Radio Receiver	.4	2,000¥	Legal	2/24 hrs	.8
Telephone	.5	3,700¥	Legal	3/24 hrs	.9
Ears					
Cyber Replacement	.3	4,000¥	Legal	2/24 hrs	.75
Modification	.1	2,000¥	Legal	2/24 hrs	1
Cosmetic Modification	—	1,000¥	Legal	2/24 hrs	.8
Hearing Amplification	.2	3,500¥	Legal	4/48 hrs	1.25
Damper	.1	3,500¥	Legal	4/48 hrs	1.25
High Frequency	.2	3,000¥	Legal	4/48 hrs	1.25
Low Frequency	.2	3,000¥	Legal	4/48 hrs	1.25
Select Sound Filter					
(Levels 1–5)	.2	Level x 10,000¥	Legal	6/48 hrs	1.25
Recorder	.3	7,000¥	12P-CA	8/48 hrs	2
Eyes					
Cyber Replacement	.2	5,000¥	Legal	2/24 hrs	.75
Camera	.4	5,000¥	Legal	6/24 hrs	2
Cosmetic Modification	—	1,000¥	Legal	2/24 hrs	.75
Vision Magnification					
Optical 1	.2	2,500¥	Legal	4/48 hrs	1
Optical 2	.2	4,000¥	Legal	4/48 hrs	1
Optical 3	.2	6,000¥	Legal	4/48 hrs	1
Electronic 1	.1	3,500¥	Legal	5/48 hrs	1
Electronic 2	.1	7,500¥	Legal	5/48 hrs	1
Electronic 3	.1	11,000¥	Legal	5/48 hrs	1
Rangefinder	.1	2,000¥	Legal	8/48 hrs	1.5
Flare Compensation	.1	2,000¥	Legal	5/48 hrs	1.25
Low-Light	.2	3,000¥	Legal	4/36 hrs	1.25
Retinal Duplication	.1	50,000+¥	3-CA	12/7 days	2
Thermographic	.2	3,000¥	Legal	4/36 hrs	1.25

	Essence Cost	Price	Legality	Availability	Street Index
INTERNALS					
Chemical Analyzer	.2	2,500¥/Level	Legal	4/6 days	1
Cortex Bomb	—	500,000¥	2-CC	20/14 days	1
Memory	Mp/100	Mp x 100¥	Legal	2/24 hrs	1
Memory (FIFF)	Mp/300	Mp x 150¥	Legal	3/24 hrs	.8
Datasoft Link	.1	1,000¥	Legal	3/24 hrs	1
Display Link	.1	1,000¥	Legal	4/36 hrs	1
Data Lock	.2	1,000¥	Legal	6/36 hrs	1.5
Data Filter	.3	5,000¥	Legal	6/36 hrs	1.5
Encephalon					
Level 1	.5	15,000¥	Legal	6/12 days	2
Level 2	.75	40,000¥	Legal	6/12 days	2
Level 3	1.5	75,000¥	Legal	6/12 days	2
Level 4	1.75	115,000¥	Legal	6/12 days	2
Gas Spectrometer	.2	2,000¥/Level	Legal	4/5 days	1
Internal Voice Mask	.1	7,000¥	6-CA	6/48 hrs	1
Olfactory Booster	.2	1,000¥/Level	Legal	6/8 days	1
Orientation System	.5	15,000¥	Legal	5/6 days	1.5
Sense Link	2	300,000¥	10P-CA	2/5 days	1
Internal Transmitter	.6	80,000¥	8P-CA	3/5 days	1.5
SPU: Data Management					
Level 1	.1	9,500¥	Legal	6/60 hrs	1
Level 2	.15	19,000¥	Legal	6/60 hrs	1
Level 3	.2	28,500¥	Legal	6/60 hrs	1
Level 4	.25	38,000¥	Legal	6/60 hrs	1
SPU: Input/Output					
Level 1	.1	5,000¥	Legal	5/4 days	1.5
Level 2	.15	7,500¥	Legal	5/4 days	1.5
Level 3	.2	12,500¥	Legal	5/4 days	1.5
Level 4	.25	22,500¥	Legal	5/4 days	1.5
SPU: Math					
Level 1	.1	2,000¥	Legal	6/60 hrs	1
Level 2	.15	5,000¥	Legal	6/60 hrs	1
Level 3	.2	11,000¥	Legal	6/60 hrs	1
Level 4	.25	23,000¥	Legal	6/60 hrs	1
Tactical Computer					
Level 1	3.5	350,000¥	4-CB	12/60 days	4
Level 2	4	900,000¥	4-CC	12/60 days	4
Level 3-4	**CLASSIFIED**	2-CC	**CLASSIFIED**		
Video Link	.5	22,000¥	Legal	4/48 hrs	1
Internal Transmitter	.4	4,500¥	Legal	6/48 hrs	1
MATRIXWARE					
MPCP	See Text	See Text	4-CD	12/60 days	4
Persona Module	.3	See Text	4-CD	Varies/12 days	Varies
Hardening	.3	See Text	4-CD	Varies/8 days	Varies
Memory/Storage	Mp/300	Mp x 150¥	Legal	3/24 hrs	.8
Transfer	.1	See Text	4-CD	Varies/10 days	Varies
Response	.2	See Text	4-CD	Varies/14 days	Varies

	Essence Cost	Price	Legality	Availability	Street Index
BODYWARE					
Hydraulic Jack					
(Levels 1–6)	.25	Level x 5,000¥	Legal	5/6 days	1
Muscle Replacement					
(Maximum Level 4)	Level	Level x 20,000¥	5P-CB	4/4 days	1
Program Carrier	.2	25,000¥	3-CD	4/48 hrs	1
Smartgun Link	.5	2,500¥	5P-CA	3/36 hrs	1
Bone Lacing					
Plastic	.5	7,500¥	6P-CA	5/14 days	1.5
Aluminum	1.15	25,000¥	6P-CB	5/14 days	1.5
Titanium	2.25	75,000¥	6-CC	5/14 days	1.5
Dermal Plating					
Level 1	.5	6,000¥	6P-CA	4/12 days	1
Level 2	1	15,000¥	6P-CA	4/12 days	1
Level 3	1.5	45,000¥	5P-CA	4/12 days	1
Filtration Systems					
Air	Level/10	Level x 15,000¥	Legal	6/4 days	1
Blood	Level/5	Level x 10,000¥	Legal	6/4 days	1
Ingested Toxin	Level/5	Level x 10,000¥	Legal	6/4 days	1
Limbs					
Simple Replacement	1	50,000¥	Legal	4/48 hrs	1
Cyber Limb	1	100,000¥	Legal	4/4 days	1
Increased Strength	—	Level x 150,000¥	6P-CA	6/4 days	1.5
Built-In Smartgun Link	.25	2,500¥	5P-CA	6/4 days	1.5
Built-In Device	—	4 x Normal Cost	Varies	Varies	Varies
Cyber Guns					
Hold-Out Pistol	.15	250¥	8P-CB + E	8/7 days	2
Light Pistol	.35	650¥	6P-CB + E	8/7 days	2
Machine Pistol	.4	900¥	4-CB + G	8/7 days	2
Submachine Gun	.6	1,800¥	3-CB + G	8/7 days	2
Heavy Pistol	1.	800¥	4P-CB + E	8/7 days	2
Shotgun	1.1	1,200¥	4P-CB + E	8/7 days	2
Skill Hardwires					
Level 1–4	Level x .2	Level x 5,000¥	Legal	6/10 days	1
Level 5–8	Level x .25	Level x 50,000¥	6P-CB	12/14 days	1.5
Level 9–10	Level x .3	Level x 500,000¥	4P-CB	12/14 days	1.5
Skillwires					
Level 1–3	Level x .1	Level x 10,000¥	Legal	4/10 days	1
Level 4–6	Level x .2	Level x 100,000¥	6P-CB	5/10 days	1
Level 7–9	Level x .3	Level x 1,000,000 ¥	4P-CB	12/20 days	1
Skillwire Plus					
Level 1–3	Level x .1	Level x 15,000¥	Legal	4/10 days	1
Level 4–6	Level x .2	Level x 125,000¥	6P-CB	5/10 days	1
Level 7–9	Level x .3	Level x 1,000,000 ¥	4P-CB	12/20 days	1
Vehicle Control Rig					
Level 1	2	12,000¥	6P-CA	6/48 hrs	1
Level 2	3	60,000¥	6P-CA	8/48 hrs	1.25
Level 3	5	300,000¥	5P-CA	8/48 hrs	1.5
Boosted Reflexes					
Level 1	.5	15,000¥	8P-CB	3/24 hrs	1
Level 2	1.25	40,000¥	6P-CB	3/24 hrs	1.25
Level 3	2.8	90,000¥	5P-CB	3/24 hrs	1.5
Wired Reflexes					
Level 1	2	55,000¥	5P-CB	4/8 days	1
Level 2	3	165,000¥	4P-CB	4/8 days	1
Level 3	5	500,000¥	3-CC	8/14 days	1

	Body Index	Base Price	Legality	Availability	Street Index
BIOWARE					
Platelet Factory	.4	30,000¥	Legal	5/8 days	1.5
Symbiotes					
Level 1	.4	15,000¥	Legal	5/10 days	1
Level 2	.7	35,000¥	Legal	5/10 days	1
Level 3	1	60,000¥	Legal	5/10 days	1
Synthacardium					
Level 1	.2	6,000¥	Legal	4/10 days	1.5
Level 2	.3	15,000¥	Legal	4/10 days	1.5
Orthoskin					
Level 1	.5	25,000¥	5P-BA	8/8 days	.8
Level 2	1	60,000¥	5P-BA	8/8 days	.8
Level 3	1.5	100,000¥	5P-BA	8/8 days	.8
Tailored Pheromones					
Level 1	.4	20,000¥	Legal	12/14 days	2
Level 2	.6	45,000¥	Legal	12/14 days	2
Adrenal Pump					
Level 1	1.25	60,000¥	5P-BB	10/16 days	3
Level 2	2.5	100,000¥	5P-BB	10/16 days	3
Suprathyroid Gland	1.4	50,000¥	6P-BB	8/12 days	2.5
Toxin Extractor	.2/Level	24,000¥/Level	Legal	4/4 days	1
Pathogenic Defense	.2/Level	24,000¥/Level	Legal	4/4 days	1.5
Cerebral Booster					
Level 1	.4	50,000¥	Legal	6/14 days	2
Level 2	.8	110,000¥	Legal	6/14 days	2
Damage Compensator					
Level 1–2	.2/Level	25,000¥/Level	6P-BA	6/6 days	2.5
Level 3–5	.2/Level	50,000¥/Level	6P-BA	10/6 days	2.
Level 6–9	.2/Level	100,000¥/Level	6P-BA	12/6 days	2.5
Mnemonic Enhancer	.2/Level	15,000¥/Level	Legal	6/7 days	1
Pain Editor	.6	60,000¥	6P-BA	6/6 days	1.2
Reflex Recorder					
Concentration	.1*	10,000¥*	Legal	5/6 days	1.5
General	.25*	25,000¥*	Legal	8/6 days	1.5
Synaptic Accelerator					
Level 1	.3	75,000¥	5P-BB	6/12 days	2
Level 2	1.6	200,000¥	5P-BB	6/12 days	2
Trauma Damper	.4	40,000¥	6P-BA	6/8 days	2
Nephritic Screen	.4	20,000¥	Legal	4/4 days	1
Extended Volume					
Level 1	.2	8,000¥	Legal	4/4 days	1
Level 2	.3	15,000¥	Legal	4/4 days	1
Level 3	.4	25,000¥	Legal	4/4 days	1
Toxin Exhaler	.6	30,000¥+	5-BB	10/4 days	3
Tracheal Filter	.2/Level	30,000¥/Level	Legal	4/4 days	1
Enhanced Articulation	.6	40,000¥	Legal	5/6 days	1.5
Muscle Augmentation	.8/Level	45,000¥/Level	4P-BC/D	6/6 days	.9

* More valuable data will cost more.

Skillsofts

	Concealability	Base Price	Legality	Availability	Street Index
Knowsoft	24	Mp x 150¥	Legal	5/4 days	1.25
Activesoft	24	Mp x 100¥	Legal	6/4 days	1.25
Linguasoft	24	Mp x 50¥	Legal	6/36 hrs	1.25
Datasoft	24	Mp x 100¥*	Legal	4/4 days	1.25

*More valuable data will cost more.

GENE-TECH

	Base Price	Legality	Availability	Street Index
Gene Therapy				
Cleansing	50,000¥	Legal	6/30 days	2.5
Genetic Correction	60,000¥	Legal	6/30 days	2.5
Reconstruct/Healing	100,000¥	Legal	6/30 days	2.5
Other	50,000¥+	Legal	6/30 days	2.5
Immunization				
Single	40,000¥ per treatment	Legal	6/20 days	2
Full Spectrum	300,000¥	Legal	6/20 days	2
Leónization	2,000,000¥ + 100,000¥	Legal	6/30 days	2.5
Antibac				
Level 1–3	Level x 500¥	Legal	4/48 hrs	1
Level 4–6	Level x 1,000¥	Legal	4/48 hrs	1
Level 7–9	Level x 1,500¥	Legal	4/48 hrs	1
Level 10+	Level x 2,500¥	Legal	4/48 hrs	1
Binder				
Level 1–3	Level x 300¥	Legal	4/32 hrs	2
Level 4–6	Level x 600¥	Legal	4/32 hrs	2
Level 7–9	Level x 900¥	Legal	4/32 hrs	2
Level 10+	Level x 1,500¥	Legal	4/32 hrs	2
Zeta-Interpheron				
Level 1–3	Level x 400¥	Legal	4/32 hrs	2
Level 4–6	Level x 800¥	Legal	4/32 hrs	2
Level 7–9	Level x 1,200¥	Legal	4/32 hrs	2
Level 10+	Level x 2,000¥	Legal	4/32 hrs	2
Doom	500¥/dose	1-M3	14/30 days	5
Gamma-Anthrax	180¥/dose	2-M3	14/30 days	6
Myco-Protein	25¥/kg	Legal	It's everywhere	1

COMPOUNDS

	Base Price	Legality	Availability	Street Index
Carcerands	See Text	Legal	4/10 days	2
Dikote™	1,000¥/100cm³	Legal	6/14 days	10
DMSO	10¥+	Legal	2/12 hrs	1.5
Oxygenated Flourocarbons	750¥ per liter	Legal	4/48 hrs	1
Ruthenium Polymers	10,000¥/m² +	Legal	5/14 days	7.5
ACTH	100¥/6 doses	Legal	5/12 hrs	1
Atropine	600¥/dose	Legal	5/12 hrs	1
Cyanide	360¥/dose	Legal	3/48 hrs	.5
Hyper	180¥/dose	4-M1	4/24 hrs	.9
Kamikaze	50¥/dose	3-M1	5/4 days	5
MAO	280¥/dose	4-M1	5/36 hrs	2

EQUIPMENT INDEX

BIOWARE
Adrenal Pump
Cerebral Booster
Damage Compensator
Enhanced Articulation
Extended Volume
Mnemonic Enhancer
Muscle Augmentation
Nephritic Screen
Orthoskin
Pain Editor
Pathogenic Defense
Platelet Factories
Reflex Recorder
Suprathyroid Gland
Symbiotes
Synaptic Accelerator
Synthacardium
Tailored Pheromones
Toxin Exhaler
Toxin Extractor
Tracheal Filter
Trauma Damper

CYBERWARE
Bone Lacing
Chemical Analyzer
Datajack
Encephalon
Gas Spectrometer
Hardening
Hydraulic Jack
Memory
Memory/Storage
MPCP
Olfactory Booster
Orientation System

Persona Module
Response
Skillsofts
Skillwire Plus
Softlink
SPU (Data Management)
SPU (Input/Output)
SPU (Math)
Tactical Computer
Transfer

GENE-TECH
Antibac
Binder
Doom
Gamma-Anthrax
Gene Therapy and Cellular Reconstruction
Immunization
Leónization
Myco-protein
Zeta-Interferon

COMPOUNDS
ACTH
Ares Squirt
Atropine
Carcerands
Cyanide
Dikote™
DMSO
Hyper
Kamikaze
Oxygenated Fluorocarbons
Ruthenium Polymers
MAO

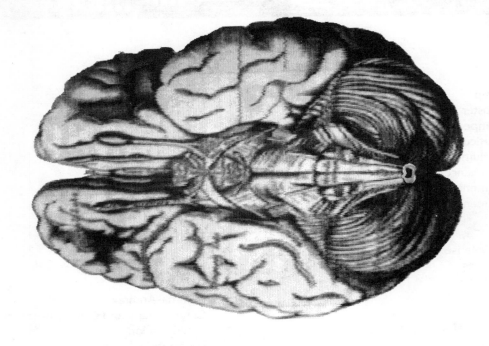